MANIC

By

Mark Brownlee

To Mum

Without your support this book would never have been published.

Copyright © 2023 by Mark Brownlee.

All rights reserved. No part of this book may be used or reproduced in any form whatsoever without written permission except in the case of brief quotations in critical articles or reviews.

This book is a work of fiction. Names, characters, businesses, organizations, places, events and incidents either are the product of the author's imagination or are used fictitiously. Any resemblance to actual persons, living or dead, events, or locales is entirely coincidental.

Printed in the United Kingdom.

For more information, or to book an event, contact :
(contact@bluesmaniac.com)
http://www.bluesmaniac.com

Book design by Kindlepreneur
Cover design by Bookcoverzone

ISBN: 9798852905635

First Edition: November 2023

CONTENTS

1 GENSIS 1

2 HOSPITAL 9

3 THE CHASE 18

4 THE ENCOUNTER 27

5 WRATH 35

6 VERITAS 45

7 THE EPISODE 54

8 AFTERMATH 60

9 CARPE DIEM 67

10 COUP D'ETAT 75

11 THE GIRL 84

12 DAY TRIP 94

13 CHRISTMAS DAY 102

14 DESPAIR 109

MANIC

15 RECOVERY 118

16 EXODUS 127

17 LOSING IT 133

18 MR EDWARDS 139

19 AKATHISIA 145

20 HUGS NOT DRUGS 154

21 MESSIAH 159

22 GETHSEMANE 165

23 THE STRANGER 171

24 CALVARY 179

25 THE RETURN 186

26 REVELATIONS 195

27 THE PERFECT GUY AND GIRL 202

28 LEAVING 210

29 THE END OF THE BEGINNING 216

ABOUT THE AUTHOR 223

ACKNOWLEDGEMENTS 224

1

GENSIS

Wednesday 18th December

"The nukes. The nukes are coming. God, please, save me."

He has abandoned me. There's a pounding in my ears. Where am I? I'm at home. In the kitchen. Must ground myself. There's Mum. Look at her. She's scared. Must be because I'm screaming. But I can't help it and the words are still spilling out.

"Rot in Hell. Go to Hell. I did nothing."

Get out of my head, my once hero, now traitor, betrayer, Judas Iscariot.

Niamh covers her mouth with her hand. "Niall?" she whispers. "Please stop screaming."

There are tears in her eyes but I have been wronged, sold for thirty pieces of silver. Why can't she see that? Why can't

MANIC

Mum see that? Why can't any of them see?

There's a hole opening up inside me. A chasm. I'm falling ... falling.

I open my eyes, remembering fragments of the things I said. "I don't know what came over me," I say, lying on the kitchen floor. It's cold on my palms. There's still a strong smell of garlic from our evening meal and there's a coppery taste in my mouth. I'm exhausted from all the screaming and what must now be the worst psychotic episode to date. I sit up and look around. There's a constant drip from the sink as my mum places a hand on my shoulder.

"Niall, it's okay," she says, trying to catch my stare.

"I thought I was going to die," I say as I look at her.

"Niall, there are two nurses who would like to talk to you. You haven't been feeling the best of late, and we wonder if you've been taking your tablets. They're waiting for you in the living room."

I struggle up from the kitchen floor. My hands are tightly locked to my forehead. I complain of a fuzziness in my brain but I'm no longer screaming which no doubt scared my family. I find my bearings in the kitchen. There are dirty dishes and some leftover dinner on the table. My family are all staring at me, with hands on their chests, thanking God.

"He's finally come to his senses," my sister Niamh whispers.

I make my way into the living room where two women in normal clothes are sitting on the sofa by the Christmas tree. One is overweight and has a no-nonsense look about her; the other is young, skinny and seems more reserved. I take a chair beside the door. There's a roaring fire that makes me rub my brow. Above the fireplace is a framed painting of the Sacred Heart of Jesus Christ which I stare at for a time. Then I turn towards the two nurses and smile, but neither respond. Their faces are serious and professional.

The overweight woman turns to me. "Good evening, Niall. We're both psychiatric nurses and we've been called in to talk to you about what happened tonight. After we'll bring your mum and dad in and ask them about it too. So, can you please tell us, first of all, your full name and age?" she says, starting to take notes.

"My name is Niall Alexander. I'm seventeen."

"And do you know where you are right now, Niall?"

Wow, they must deal with real crazy people if one of their introductory questions is asking someone where they are.

"I'm in my living room," I reply, wondering if I get a Blue Peter badge for answering correctly.

"And do you know what day it is?"

I'm tempted to say Christmas Day 17 AD and I'm the Messiah, but they'll probably admit me to hospital for sure and I definitely don't want that.

"It's Wednesday 18th December."

"Now, what I want you to do is slowly take us through what happened today."

"Ah." What do I say? The truth. I guess I can't get out of this one because there are too many witnesses. "I thought the house was going to be nuked by the US government," I say, stumbling over my words. Yeah, I know it sounds crazy now but it made perfect sense at the time.

The nurse who spoke frowns and rubs her chin but continues to question me. "And why did you think the US government was going to destroy your house?"

"You've probably heard in the news about Christa Edwards' suicide attempt. I was horrified. I always admired her commitment to tackling climate change and other social issues," I say, clutching my thumbs with my fingers. Yeah, and because she is smoking hot, too, but I don't say that. "I needed to do something to help her recover from her depression. The world needs people like her to give us hope. So, I started writing letters to her, then some to her dad."

The main nurse still frowns. "James Edwards? You were writing letters to the President of the United States of America?"

"Yeah, but I didn't send any. I started to create a collection of letters, emails and scripts and planned phone calls to get him to come to my house." Sounds kinda lame and stupid but at the time I thought I could get him to come to my house for Christmas Day.

3

MANIC

"Why did you want to meet him? I thought you wanted to help Christa?"

Weeelll … yeah, that's partly true. How do I say this without sounding like a creep? I mean I do have a crush on her. I clear my throat and continue. "I watched the movie *Taken* last night for the first time, and that scared the life out of me." I turn to the nurse again. "I thought Edwards was going to hunt me down and kill me, like Bryan Mills in the movie, when I came home from school. I kept looking out of the window, expecting all manner of military hardware and personnel to come and take me away."

Just to make sure she doesn't think I'm really crazy, I don't tell her that I thought the CIA had tapped my phone and were monitoring my computer. Oh yeah, and that Edwards was reading my mind.

The main nurse leans forward. "Have you been taking your medication?"

"Yes," I say unconvincingly. I decide to lie this time. If I said no, they'd definitely throw me into the Psych ward for sure. Alarm bells always ring when you tell people you haven't been taking your medication. I haven't taken any for the past four days, and I haven't slept. I've been staying up all night trying to write letters to Edwards.

"And have you consumed any alcohol lately?" she continues.

"I'm underage."

"Just checking," she says. "What about any illegal substances?"

"No, I've never taken any drugs." Honestly, I've always been sober when it comes to the hard stuff.

She glances up at me when she finishes. "That's fine, Niall. We'll now have a conversation with your parents."

I go along the hall into my bedroom and stand before my wardrobe. It's open with unironed shirts hanging over its doors. I go to my bookshelf and caress the spine of my Jerusalem Bible then look at the book box set of Dante's *Divine Comedy* beside it. If I am going to the hospital, I'll be bringing these with me. I reverently take a crucifix hanging by my bed. I kiss the body of Christ and then place the rosary into my pocket before one of

MARK BROWNLEE

the nurses comes into my room.

She stares at me. "Niall, can you please come into the living room again? I would like to talk to you with the rest of your family."

I feel a sudden knot in my stomach. My throat feels constricted and my mouth goes dry. I quickly pray to every saint I know that I will not be chucked into the hospital. I stand in a corner of the living room, clutching my elbows with my hands. I look at the nurse's face. It doesn't look good. She looks around the room at all the family members gathered. Dad is sitting in his usual seat with Mum standing over him. If we were a half-functioning family she would be sitting on the side of the armchair, with her arm around him. But we're not and so she's not.

The nurse clears her throat. "I think it's in Niall's best interests that he is admitted to a psychiatric hospital."

No! My pulse races and I clench my jaw. What is everybody in school going to think? "A psychiatric hospital? You mean I'll be living with mindless nutjobs and psychopathic killers?"

"Niall!" Mum shouts.

"The hospital you're going to is for children and adolescents so you will be living with people your own age and I can assure you it will be a safe place that will help you get better."

"But I don't need to get better. I'm fine now," I say, looking around at everybody who are unable to hold my gaze and say nothing. Mental hospital? Can I deal with that? Will they put me in a straightjacket? Lock me up in a padded cell or zap me with electro-convulsive shocks just to get a kick out of it? I've been unwell before but they've always treated me with medication after consulting a psychiatrist. Today's different. I might be entering a mental hospital for the first time and I don't know if I can handle that.

Mum breaks the silence. "Niall, the best place for you right now is in the hospital," she says, rubbing the bruise Dad gave her yesterday, now covered over. After all, there are visitors present. Then I realise home isn't exactly a utopia in comparison.

MANIC

"Alright," I say, surprising myself that I even managed to utter the word. But this isn't the end of the story. If things get too hairy, I'm confident I can twist my mum's arm and persuade her to bring me home.

Mum, Dad, Conor and Niamh all get into the car. We drive down the lane leading to our old house. We are flanked on both sides by orchards. A few rays of light allow us to observe the great veins and capillaries of trees in the dead of winter. I have just gone through a near-death experience. Yeah, totally delusional, but it felt like a near-death experience, even though in reality, I was in no danger.

"Sssooo, how do you feel now?" Conor asks awkwardly.

I nod and smile. "Better." After all, Edwards isn't actually after me. But a part of me wants to think that he is, just to bask in a sense of significance. I'm breathing normally; I sigh out of exhaustion. The episode was a real drain of energy. All the paranoia has passed, I'm relieved and I perceive life in a totally new way. Was the episode, or how I feel now, a profound religious experience? No. But I want it to be, and somehow my desire makes it so. I had and I'm currently having, a religious experience, a baptism of fire. An experience as deep and as meaningful as Teresa of Avila's vision of the angel piercing her heart. All I want to do now is live a life of service to God. There is a sense in my mind that the Almighty is currently saying to me the same words he said to Christ at his baptism: *"This is my Son, the Beloved; my favour rests on him."* Yet if I truly am the Son of God, what can I expect of my life now?

As the car turns, I look down to the GAA club. If it wasn't for it, my parents never would have met at that evening dance. At the time Mum was studying English and Dad had started lecturing Classics at Queens. Apparently, he was a charmer in his day before he hit the bottle.

As we get closer to the hospital an idea fixates in my head. "James Edwards and his daughter Christa are in the hospital."

"Niall, I'm pretty sure James Edwards and his daughter are in the White House," Conor says.

MARK BROWNLEE

But I'm right. "Edwards is in this very hospital. Christa is here, clinically depressed, but I can help her get better."

"Niall, this is just one of your weird delusions," Conor says.

Dad cynically tilts his head back. Trust him to show any sympathy.

Mum looks back at Conor through the rear-view mirror. "We can be a bit more sensitive about your brother's condition."

"Sorry. But he was like this the last time he was unwell. Remember?" Conor says. "You had that sudden urge to become a priest. You even wrote to Father Doyle telling him to resign as you thought you would do a better job running the parish."

We suddenly skid on a patch of ice. I clutch Mum's seat in front of me to support myself. Niamh jolts into Conor. Mum manages to steady the vehicle. We find a parking space in front of the hospital. Dad turns to Mum and nods then we walk slowly to the entrance.

I clutch Conor by the arm and stare at him dead in the eyes. "I'm telling you, Edwards and Christa are in this very building. We'll meet them soon." My heart races at the prospect of meeting my hero. I know what you're thinking. How is he my hero if I was comparing him to Judas Iscariot earlier? It's simple, really. Even though everybody else thinks I need to go to the hospital, the fact that I view Edwards as my hero now is proof that I'm perfectly fine and sane again.

I take a close look at the place – a run-down concrete box. It's a dive. It has horrible cement walls of the most depressing hue. How's that meant to be conducive to lifting somebody out of a deep depression or any mental illness?

Mum turns around and offers me a hand. "Niall, it's for the best."

"Hopefully, this place will do the trick," Dad says. Yeah, like he knows or even cares.

I stand in the pouring rain and stare at the entrance.

The rain soaks me to the skin and I shiver at the sound of thunder while drops of water run into my clenched fists. Mum presses the button to reception. A voice comes from the speakers.

"Serenity Juvenile Psychiatric Hospital. Christine speaking. How can I help?"

"It's Siobhan Alexander. I'm here to bring Niall."

"Okay."

The door unlocks with a buzz and we push it open to what will be a brand-new experience for me. For better or worse, I'm not quite sure yet.

2

HOSPITAL

Wednesday 18th December

We walk into the lobby area. I stare at the health posters on the wall and glass panes in the reception room. It's unoccupied, but something catches my attention. The architectural plan of the hospital has strange semi-circle shapes like something out of a sci-fi movie. People are being paged over the intercom and there is the whoosh of the automatic doors as visitors come through the main entrance.

A nurse with brown hair with a pen stuck in the back of her ponytail makes her way along the corridor towards us in an immaculate pale blue uniform that says this woman means business. She looks at me.

"You must be Niall. Follow me. I'm Christine. I'll be one of

MANIC

the nurses looking after you during your stay," she says in a Southern Irish accent.

I'm taken aback by the conditions of the hospital. Everything seems to be ordered by strict utility but the smell of alcohol stirs my stomach and makes me want to retch. Am I about to be part of a social experiment against my will or like some alien probed in Area 51? I walk along the corridor which leads to a ward. We stop and stand outside the double doors. Christine removes her key card from her waist and scans it to open the door. It beeps as she allows us to enter.

In the ward the walls are beige and there is a large abstract mosaic opposite the medication room. What is it? I'm not sure. Is it some kind of outline of a brain? Mental, if you ask me but then again, I'm in a mental hospital. There's a strong smell of astringent hand sanitiser and bleach as a cleaner mops the floor. I hear the automated hum as sanitiser is dispensed from a machine and there's a scent of latex gloves as a nurse puts on PPE.

Christine brings me to a room of very basic and bland furniture. Most of the furnishings are chipped around the edges. She then tells me to wait in the TV room as she talks to my family. There's a whiteboard with patient information and a large window with its blinds pulled. The television is situated in the corner of the room. I set my wallet on the table and sit quietly, frowning.

This place isn't quite Hell but it certainly is some kind of Purgatory. My heart races and my limbs shake slightly when I think of how long I'll be here. Soon my family come in to see me. Mum immediately notices my wallet on the table and alerts me to it. But I merely shrug. She probably thinks of the last time I was high. I went with a friend to Tesco's and bought a carload of Mountain Dew with her card. She takes the wallet off the table and says she will give me weekly allowances of cash while I'm in the hospital.

She kisses me. "Goodbye, Niall. Don't worry. I'll visit you as often as I can. Oh, I have something for you."

She takes a book out of her bag and hands it to me. Mum, forever the English teacher, wants me to read something while I'm here.

MARK BROWNLEE

"Give me a break. I'm not at school."

"I know, but you are going through a very formative point in your life. I think it would be good for you to read this."

I sigh and look at the cover of the book. *A Portrait of the Artist as a Young Man* by James Joyce. Joyce? Mum's favourite, I could have guessed. After all, she immerses us in *Ulysses* every June 16th for Bloomsday.

I paste on a smile and take the book. "I'll be fine," I say but I'm scared whether I'll survive in this place. There's a looseness in my bladder and my heart races. I really don't want her to leave.

She frowns and Conor shakes my hand. "Yeah, you'll be fine, Niall. You hear?"

"Yeah. I hope so."

My sister Niamh briefly wraps her arms around me. "I hope you get well soon here."

She offers me a green cross, woven out of rushes.

"It's the cross of Saint Brigid. I got it at the holy well in Kildare. She's the patron saint of healers you know. It'll help you get better."

I nod. It'll take more than a holy relic to make me feel better but at least her heart's in the right place.

Dad shakes my hand. "Alright, Niall. All the best. You hopefully won't be here too long." Daniel Alexander, always one for making situations more awkward than they already are.

When they leave, I remain in the seating area outside the staff base. The wooden seat is so hard that it doesn't take long for my ass to get sore. Christine comes out and with a smile, gestures to me to see the psychiatrist. I have a question on my mind. Are James and Christa Edwards in the building? But I want to be subtle.

"Are there any American patients on this ward?"

Christine shakes her head.

I sigh. I guess this isn't going to be the evening I meet the leader of the free world and his hot daughter.

"Have you any more questions?" she adds, as a door bangs and a patient screams.

Yeah, one definitely comes to mind after that. "Do you ..." I rub the back of my neck, "you know, use straightjackets

MANIC

here?"

Christine smiles. "The days of using straightjackets in places like this are long gone." She peers down at her notes then looks at me again with a smile. It's infectious as I end up smiling. Not that my fears of being in this place have changed but I feel more at ease around Christine.

I enter the room with an empty feeling in my stomach and the doctor is sitting behind a pine coffee table. There is a large artificial plant to his right. He's in his forties, bald, overweight with glasses. He wears a formal suit and his black trousers have two long creases down the middle. I'm aware of white coat syndrome which is where you're fearful of medical professionals and I know I don't have it. Still, I'm sitting not too far away from the man who is the king of this castle. If I have any desire to leave his dungeon, I'll need to play ball. But can I trust him?

He's big in all respects and has a warm and sincere glint in his eyes, which causes an unexpected release of tension. I sit on my armchair with a nervous demeanour. I tap the floor with my foot which I'm sure annoys him, not that I mean to but he seems to retain his composure anyway. I stare at him.

"Good evening, Niall. I'm Doctor Henson and I will be your psychiatrist for the duration of your stay in the hospital," he says in a Welsh accent.

He pauses for a moment. "Can you tell me a bit about how you managed to end up here?"

His tone of voice is remarkably calm and makes me sigh and ease into my chair. I smile and find myself saying, "Are you familiar with *The Lord of the Rings* trilogy, Doctor?"

"Actually, Niall, I'm not."

"Well, my American cousin Bradley provided me with a rather insightful modern interpretation of it."

"Does this relate to what happened to you today?"

"Of course." Although it probably has more to do with the fact that I recently read the books which ended up being part of the fodder of my manic episode at home.

"Well then, go on," he says, repositioning himself in his seat.

"In *The Lord of the Rings* there are five peoples who are

the main forces for good and there are two who are the main forces for evil. You have Elves, high-cultured beings who don't do much. Does that remind you of a modern group of people?"

"Actually, I can't say that it does."

"The French? Then there's the Dwarves, industrious, serious people, who lack a sense of humour – the Germans? Then you have humans, split into the kingdoms of Rohan and Gondor. The people of Gondor are a proud people because they once enjoyed greater glory – the British? The people of Rohan are warm-hearted but uncivilised – the Americans? And last, but not least, my favourite group of people from the trilogy – the Hobbits. A parochial yet well-humoured group of people who are pacifists at heart, so long as they're not drunk or the fight's In their backyard." I notice Doctor Henson is smiling. "Yes, that's right, the Irish." For all you diehard Lord of the Ring fans out there thinking Tolkien despised it when people allegorised his work, well, so what!

"And who are the forces of evil?" he asks.

"Isengard and Mordor or China and Russia." Duh, you're meant to be the doctor, man.

"Niall, I believe you experienced a very traumatic episode today. Was it because you believed that Russia and China were after you?"

"No, I thought the President of the United States was after me." Not anymore though, which is a relief.

"The United States? Isn't it a force for good, according to your interpretation?"

"Yeah, it is. I thought James Edwards was coming to get me. He's the great king of Rohan. But when I was manic, I thought I was Grima Wormtongue, a pawn of Isengard and a worker of evil. I thought, in his wrath, he would kill me but he didn't."

"So, you're not this Grima Wormtongue. Then who are you?"

The existential question that every man, woman and child must ask themselves – who are we? Sorry, I'm getting distracted.

"Well, I'm Irish and therefore a hobbit. The hobbits are kind of the main characters in Lord of the Rings. Frodo, the

MANIC

main one, has the ring of power that everybody wants."

"So, you're Frodo. Do you want to be as powerful as James Edwards with the ring?"

"What? Of course not. I'm Tom Bombadil, the one who the ring has no effect on, probably because he pushed above his weight and bagged a hot elven chick called Goldberry. You can let Edwards deal with Russia and China. I mean, I'm only seventeen. All I want is a hot chick who will treat me right." Henson nods at me.

"You know, Doctor, you remind me of Hannibal," I say.

"So, I'm a cannibal, am I?"

"Of course not. You're a psychopath. All the best surgeons, bankers and psychiatrists are psychopaths." I'm not sure if I've just complimented or insulted him.

"So, I'm a psychopath like Hannibal Lecter?"

"Oh, no. Hannibal Barca, the Carthaginian general who took on Rome. But yeah, he also was a psychopath too. I mean, he led his army over the Alps in winter. A genius but still something only a psychopath would do. Thankfully, for the sake of Roman civilization, he was defeated in the end."

"So, I'm the bad guy?"

"What makes you think that?"

"I'm a psychopath like Hannibal."

"There are good psychopaths and bad psychopaths."

He laughs. "I hope I'm a good one."

I nod and smile. I really hope so too, but I am still uneasy about being in this place.

When we finish, I head to my room. A guy with headphones on is in front of me in the corridor. I quicken my pace, creep up behind and tap him on the shoulder. He turns his pale face around while taking one headphone off.

"What?"

"What's your name?"

"Martin." Then he just walks on.

Knob. Clearly not the best introduction I've ever had with a stranger.

I make my way back to my room and sit at the table where I sit and fiddle with a pen for a while. The door opens and Christine appears. "Supper's ready."

MARK BROWNLEE

I stroll up to the canteen. Once there the kitchen shutters lift and out from the gap appears a man in his thirties with fair hair and a pleasant smile. He scoops out porridge into bowls. When it's my turn, I smile and say thanks and receive my portion. I turn around to find a place to sit. Martin already is at a table but there are still three remaining chairs. I set my porridge on the table and sit down. I'm followed by a guy who introduces himself as Colin Matchett. My jaw drops. I'm tall but this guy is six foot six, built like a tank with muscles in places I never knew you could have muscles. It would be an insult to say this dude was conceived, more like constructed. He's a Rugby jock, for sure, with his Ulster Rugby top on. They don't tend to treat me well at school. I mean I could take one of those Gaelic jocks in school. Yet I lack their built in aggression that means they always have to win and never give up.

"Where are you from?" he asks.

"Armagh," I say. Maybe he's not so bad. "Yourself?"

"Ballymena. So, have you any ladies on the go?" he asks with a smirk.

"No," I say with an unpleasant tingling across the back of my neck.

He gives a friendly grin at my remark.

A jock, no doubt, but I'm more comfortable around him than Martin because he seems dead on. I'm curious what sort of mental illness or condition he has got? I mean, we are all here for a reason. It must be serious, otherwise, he wouldn't be here. It's rude to ask but I can always speculate. He must fall into one of three categories: bipolarism, unipolarism or schizophrenia. Is he bipolar like me?

"So, how long have you been here, Colin?"

"I was admitted a couple of weeks ago. I had a few terrible days before coming in. My psychiatrist diagnosed me as having a personality disorder. I was pissed off when he told me that. He said, 'don't take it personal' to which I replied, 'how do you expect me not to take it personal, you've just said I'm personally disordered.'"

The canteen becomes silent until one of the male patients called Christopher, shouts, "Excuse me. But did you call me an idiot?"

MANIC

I'm surprised since nobody said anything to this guy.

When Martin and Colin finish their supper, their chairs scrape across the floor as they leave.

Martin turns to Colin. "How about a game of table tennis?" Colin agrees and both leave me on my own.

A smoking hot girl, roughly my age, comes and sits at my table, beside me. She has ginger hair at shoulder length and a skinny frame. Her face, in places, has a spot of acne, yet her complexion is mostly clear and pale. Her cheeks are full, her pink lips look soft and tender. I notice the meagre contents of food in her bowl. I want to start a conversation but I'm sweating as I usually do when I'm around girls I like. I muster the courage to speak.

"Hey there, I'm Niall."

She grins. "Stephanie."

"Have you been here long?" I add.

"Two weeks. But I've been in and out of the hospital now since I was sixteen," she says with an unnatural stillness while avoiding my gaze.

"Man, sorry to hear that."

Okay, folks. Let's sum up. Christine and Henson seem dead on. Martin strikes me as a idiot but Colin seems sound. Stephanie? Well, would a girl that good looking ever be interested in a guy like me? Honestly? I don't know but something tells me I may have a pope's chance in Heaven as opposed to a snowball's chance in Hell.

I look around the room, lean back into my chair and let out a loud sigh. There's a sudden feeling of tiredness but it is fulfilling rather than exhausting. The kind of feeling you get when the bell rings at the end of school. There's a lightness in my chest and a feeling that this place might not be as bad as I initially thought.

Christine comes over to the table. "You've still got to take your tablets."

Tablets? I haven't taken them for the past four days. Of course, that was due to absent-mindedness. Now I'm faced with the choice to take them. Should I? Will the medication not slow me down? Turn me into a vegetable? How am I supposed to get a girl like this Stephanie, or any girl for that matter, if I'm over sedated? I can't let this opportunity pass me by but what am I going to do? Now in the hospital I'm expected to comply with medication. Could I refuse? No, I will appear to conform and pretend to take medication. I grin.

I walk to the medication room, noticing it's quiet. The two nurses administering my medication are Christine and an older male nurse. He reads out my prescribed drugs and dosage while Christine drops them into a small medicine cup and hands them to me. When the nurses look away, I slide the tablets into my pocket and down a glass of water. Christine turns around and I stick my tongue out. She nods.

I go to my room and get into bed. Stephanie is on my mind before I fall asleep.

3

THE CHASE

Thursday 19th December

he next day I enter the foyer where Martin and Colin are playing table tennis. I collapse into an armchair and close my eyes. The bounce of the ping pong ball across the table is remarkably relaxing. I drift off to sleep and fantasise about living with Stephanie. We would work in the perfectly run orchards with all the other labourers, with everyone getting equal pay, work and leisure. All traces of poverty and inequality are eradicated. She's picking Victoria plums in August, wearing a sun hat and flowery dress on her perfect body. I turn my head in the armchair. Maybe we'd live on a remote Greek island where we would work the olive groves. She'd be the strong and diligent Athena, goddess of the olive grove. I sigh then sit up and open my eyes.

"So, sleeping beauty awakens. Did you have any kinky dreams?" Colin asks.

I laugh. "If I did, I wouldn't be telling you."

"Come on, we're all friends here. You were thinking about Stephanie."

I smile. How does he know this? I say nothing.

"Don't worry, mate. I'm not telepathic. I saw the way you were looking at her last night. I'll play you a game of table tennis for her."

My lip curls, disgusted at Colin's proposition. I mean, I wouldn't call myself a feminist or anything but such things are from a bygone era. Was I right to think Colin was a sound guy? I guess my first impressions were wrong.

"Wouldn't she have to agree?" I ask.

"You're right. How about a pact? The winner merely gets the privilege of asking her out first," Colin smiles while making a sexual gesture.

Okay, he is definitely a idiot like Martin. On the topic of Stephanie, I only met her last night so it's hard to tell. I feel threatened. After all, Colin strikes me as the super athletic rugby jock type that gets any girl he wants. Still, you never know, I might be more up her street.

"I think she'd be more interested in me," he says.

I stare at him. "What are you saying?"

"You're alright but … well, if Stephanie had to choose, she would choose me over you."

I can't believe this. Is Colin really better looking than me? Maybe Martin can give me some much-needed relief but I'm not holding my breath.

"Martin, what do you think? Is he better looking than me?"

He looks up from his phone, glancing at both of us. "Guys, I'd like to say off the bat that I'm not gay. So, I really can't comment."

"Is it a dualistic battle between Yin and Yang or between God and the created devil?" I ask.

"What are you talking about?" he snaps.

I sigh.

Colin grins. "If it's Yin and Yang, can I be white? I want to

MANIC

be the good guy."

I pause and then one word seems to sum up everything Colin has been arguing about and I accidentally say it aloud. "Rubbish."

Colin's quick to react. "If it's rubbish, then you've got nothing to fear. If I win the game, I ask her out first and get rejected. You've only got everything to gain. If you win the game, you keep me in check and are then free to go on and ask her out. Do you want to play?"

Finally, he's making sense. "I'll play."

"Cool."

Martin watches us take our positions around the table. We lift our bats. Colin holds the ball in his hand and smiles at me, showing his white teeth. I want to break them with a hammer.

I can't remember the last time I played table tennis. It probably was at primary school. It quickly emerges that Colin is a better player than me and it's most likely that he will win overall. But I give him a run for his money, and we have two close-fought games. He wins them both, so there's no third. After the final result, there's a pulse in my throat as my heart thuds dully in my chest,

"So that's it then. Since I won, I can ask Stephanie out first."

Stephanie is walking along the corridor towards Colin, who has his back turned to her. She is wearing a long white dress with a green trench coat over the top with dozens of badges sewn on its arms, like the peace sign and the communist hammer and sickle.

"I'm flattered, Colin. But I didn't know guys these days won over girls by playing table tennis," she says.

Thank you, Stephanie. That's exactly what I thought and you know what they say – great minds think alike. My heart rate goes up. I'm numb at the sour taste in my mouth.

"But if you had to choose?" Colin asks.

"What, so I can stroke your egos? I'll keep that to myself. But I could make things interesting for you," she says with a smile. That must mean she likes me. She's a player. This girl is playing hard to get and you can bet your bottom dollar I'm going to play along because I'm going to hit the jackpot.

"Alright how about you play me at a game of table tennis? Whoever beats me, I'll kiss them on the lips. But if I beat both of you, you have to kiss each other on the lips. How does that sound?"

I might not be the greatest table tennis player in the world, but I'm pretty sure I can beat a girl, and Colin seems to think the same, so we both agree. But even if I lose and Colin wins, I'm convinced this babe will still be after me.

Colin and I agree.

"Good. Colin first," she says.

Colin stands at one end while Stephanie takes off her trench coat, revealing a red cardigan underneath. She stands at the other end with her bat in hand.

"I warn you, I've won a few school table tennis tournaments," she says.

I take a seat beside Martin as Colin serves first. Stephanie hits back as they start a rally. My gaze follows Martin's as his head turns right and left with the play of the ball. Stephanie's serve goes straight over the netting to Colin's end. He quickly stretches over to one side where the ball is and hits it back, but he doesn't get it over the net. Perhaps not the best of starts but it doesn't seem to dampen his optimism.

"Come on, Colin. You can do it," he shouts to himself. I hope Stephanie will make him squirm. Stephanie serves and gets the point.

A thought comes to me. Why's Martin not interested in Stephanie? Although I don't want to further complicate the situation by introducing a third guy to the mix, I'm curious.

"Martin, I'm wondering if there is a special girl in your life?"

"No woman, no cry," he rallies back, his eyes fixed on the moving ball.

Colin overhears and misses the shot, erupting with laughter (point to Stephanie).

He picks the ball up. "You're a wise man, Martin. Wiser than the two of us planks."

I smile too. Maybe I misjudged Martin; maybe he's not a idiot. Colin, on the other hand, I am convinced is, with every

MANIC

passing second.

They continue with the game. Although not a lousy player, Colin is no match for Stephanie. She has lightning reflexes and an unstoppable serve. As the game progresses, Colin snatches the odd point but he is never able to take the lead. The game finishes twenty-one–thirteen to Stephanie.

"No kiss for you, I'm afraid. Now, Niall. My next victim?"

I get up from my seat, shaking slightly. What have I gotten myself into? I'm facing a beautiful, superhuman amazon with nothing more than a puny rubber fan. It's a good job we didn't agree on a French kiss. Colin might have nice teeth, but his breath has a strong, pungent stench, the type you get after eating a packet of Tayto cheese and onion crisps. Ah, he's just opened a packet of Tayto cheese and onion crisps. I guess he does not fancy my chances; I can't say I do either.

Stephanie and I face each other across the table. We have a practice rally where Stephanie is more daring, hitting harder than me. Sometimes the ball hits the net or misses my side of the table but she's near perfect to me. She swings the bat in her right hand with all the force of her body, making her flail the other arm to the left. The ball bounces across to my end before I can say 'ping pong, bang the gong'. I struggle to parry her hard-hitting serves, but since it's only a practice, I don't mind. Occasionally, my angel makes unforced errors that give me something to cling onto.

We start and sustain a long rally during which Stephanie grunts. Am I playing against Maria Sharapova? She wins many points, all after long rallies with a lot of grunting on her part. Then there are the aces and she gets a lot of aces, striking the ball so fast I can barely see it to respond. Often, my arm is fully extended as I lunge from either side of my end. Man, this is a workout. Then my service – which is a big improvement from my last, winning quite a few points. Maybe I won't have to kiss Colin after all.

Then after a marathon of a rally, I gain a point by hitting the ball at a side strike which spins to Stephanie who misses it entirely. We stop for a breather, bent over and exhausted. Stephanie is panting and I'm getting turned on.

At the minute, the score's a tie. Now it's a matter of

MARK BROWNLEE

finding out what power Stephanie's carrot and stick has over me. Realising I'm close to kissing her, removes my fear of kissing Colin but then she executes a formidable ace that I can't react to. She wins all five points of her service and wins the game. I offer her my hand to shake with a feeling of numbness and lack of energy, but she gives a cheeky smile and sticks out her tongue.

Colin puts the last of his crisps into his mouth and then licks each of his fingers. Now he's taking the piss. He stands up and faces me. Isn't this awkward? He takes a step forward. I take one back.

She laughs. "I wasn't expecting either of you to go through with it. But if you want, be my guests."

I guess we look like two right muppets. I look to Martin to see what he thinks of the whole spectacle but he's already gone on his phone.

I turn around to see Stephanie but she's not there. Colin goes off to find her. I sit over with Martin who puts his phone away.

"I don't know. You guys are crazy for her, but she made right fools of you both," he says.

I watch Colin walk along the corridor. "I know but deep down I'd say she's got a good heart. Those badges she has on her coat. I can tell she's a socialist."

"What, one of those filthy rich women with big mansions and their own TV shows?"

"No, you're thinking of a socialite. A socialist is somebody who cares for the poor."

"Whatever floats your boat, mate. I could do with a smoke. You fancy one?"

"No, but I could do with some fresh air."

We go through the canteen towards the smoking area. Outside, we find a dark-haired girl called Ramona; she asks if either of us have any grass. We both shake our heads.

When Martin and I come back inside, I spot something that intrigues me. It's Christopher, sitting at a table by himself in the canteen, finger painting. One work of three pink daisies catches my eye. I move closer to get a better view and admire his amazing work. He clearly has a real talent for it. He doesn't

MANIC

look at me; he is so engrossed in his craft.

Eventually, he looks up. "Excuse me, but did you just call me obese?" he says, peering up and around.

I frown. "Of course not. I would never say something like that."

I point to the painting of the daisies. "You see this painting here. It's fantastic."

He ignores me and works on. Colin and Stephanie come into the corridor, laughing. Maybe they've just got their antidepressants. I say nothing but feel a burning sensation in my chest as my stomach hardens and my breathing becomes coarser. Stephanie peers over at Christopher.

"Wow! Colin, have you seen this? Hey, are you interested in selling this painting of the daisies?" Stephanie asks.

"Fifty quid," Christopher yells.

Stephanie flinches.

"I'd be willing to give fifty quid for your little creation," Colin says, giving me a wink.

"Christopher, I'd be prepared to give you sixty pounds for your portrait," I say.

I can't let this scumbag Colin buy a piece of art he doesn't even like, especially if he's going to give to Stephanie.

"Guys, you don't have to do this. I can pay for it myself. I have savings."

"Sixty-five," Colin says.

I cut in. "Seventy and my watch."

"You're giving him your watch?" she says with her eyes flashing and her mouth twisted in an ugly sneer that leaves me flinching.

Christopher inspects the watch for a moment. "Deal."

I couldn't have gone much higher. I only have just over seventy quid in my bag after I gave my wallet to Mum. Thankfully I now have it in my pockets, not that I'll have much left after this purchase. I give him the money and my watch and shake Christopher's hand. I hold up the painting and marvel at its beauty and then offer it to Stephanie. She throws it on the ground and storms off.

"Yep. That's real ungrateful material right there," Martin says.

"Should one of us see if she's okay?" I ask.

Colin gestures to me along the corridor. "You're the one that bought the painting. Be my guest."

I walk along the corridor as if I'm walking the green mile. Judging how feisty and pissed Stephanie is, it could be my last mile. I reach the bottom of the corridor and look around. It's quiet. Maybe she's hiding, which could mean she doesn't want to see me. What keeps me looking is how perplexed I am at the whole situation. I just gave somebody seventy quid and my watch for a painting (granted, a good painting) but one I immediately offered to a girl who threw it on the floor. Maybe she's playing hard to get. But Princess Leia played hard to get with Han Solo in *Empire Strikes Back*, and both critics and fans agree that was the best of the original *Star Wars* trilogy. It's a shame Lucas had to mess it up in *The Return of the Jedi,* having her in that ridiculous outfit with Jabba the Hutt. I guess I like it when a girl plays hard to get.

I turn a corner. She's sitting looking out of the window and makes no reaction as I sit down beside her.

"Hey, I'm sorry," I say, trying to get her attention.

"What are you sorry for?" she snaps at me.

To be honest, I don't know, but I thought she'd at least cut me some slack for being apologetic.

"Why did you buy me that painting?"

I take a deep breath. "Because I knew you wanted it."

"Yet when I told you not to buy it, you bought it anyway."

I feel my brow wrinkle. "Yeah, I don't see the issue."

"The issue is you're like my dad."

Ah no, she's got dad issues.

"He's a businessman. He jets off all over the world but he's never home. Then at Christmas and birthdays, he thinks he's great, buying us all these expensive gifts we don't even need."

"But I bought you something you wanted."

"Did I need it? We all want different things at times, Niall. It's always important to remember what we need. Plus, you wrongly assume I'm into a guy who's got a big wallet. You win a girl by talking to her and being there for her. There's no complicated formula. Just thought I'd give you a tip on how to

MANIC

get a girl that's worth pursuing. And by the way, the kiss is still on offer but only if you happen to beat me at table tennis."

She taps me on the shoulder then leaves me.

I feel my phone vibrate in my pocket. I have a missed call from Dad and a voice message:

"Niall. It's your dad. I know your mum has already left a book for you to read in the hospital. However, my recommendation, Marcus Aurelius' Meditations, will be of more benefit to your mind. I left it at the hospital reception for you to collect. I don't need to tell you he was a stoic who wanted to keep his mind sharp when he was fighting off the barbarians of civilization and culture. It has done me an immense benefit to read it multiple times and I know it will do you the same. Get well soon.   Deo volente."

Now I've got two books to read. Why can't they see that my mind needs a rest right now?

4

THE ENCOUNTER

Thursday 19th December

walk with Stephanie up to the canteen. I barely know this person but already I have feelings for her. There isn't that much space between us as we walk. Could I hold her hand? No. Maybe? The opportunity disappears when we enter the canteen and she stands in front of me in line for food. I sit at a table with her, Martin and Colin. She smiles at me.

I'm struck at how good looking she is with her long wavy ginger hair. I try my best not to stare, but why on earth is a girl like her in the hospital? With a face like that she could go places. After a long silence, I try to strike up a conversation but I have no idea what to say. Come on, Niall. Say something, anything.

"Sooo, nirvana?"

MANIC

Nirvana? Why did you say that? Do you think you're some Tibetan monk? Hang on, maybe you can turn it around and say you're really into Kurt Cobain and pray she's into grunge.

"So, you're a follower of the eastern religions?" she says, munching on a forkful of food.

Wait, now she thinks I'm a Tibetan monk. Can those guys even marry? Best steering away from things you don't know much about.

"No," I reply. "You?"

"I'm interested in them."

Hang on, maybe I should have said I was into eastern religion.

"I'm not particularly devout. Certain Buddhist kinds of thinking make a lot of sense to me as do other religions," she says, bowing her head to eat.

"Jesus was a pretty cool guy," I say after filling my mouth with some potato. I know most people like Him even if they're not particularly devout.

Stephanie smiles. "Oh, so you're a Christian then?"

"Ah, no. Catholic." Hang on, was that the right answer?

She laughs and tilts her head back, revealing her perfectly white teeth. I'm weightless right now with sudden warmth in my insides and my stomach fluttering.

She regains her composure. "What are you studying at school?"

"Religion, History and Politics."

"Explains a lot," she says with a grin then puts on a straight face. "I didn't know they taught them as separate subjects in the North."

Right now, I feel utterly present in the moment with Stephanie as I stare into her eyes. But I need to keep this conversation going. I can't just stare at her; she'll think I'm a creep. But she's the one who continues the conversation.

"What are you studying in politics?"

I sigh. "The US constitution."

"What do you think of the current US President, James Edwards? I think he's awesome."

I can't believe my ears. She likes my hero, whom I've idolised for years. I grin. "You like him? Me too." Great, Niall.

28

You've found something in common with her. Now don't mess it up.

I smile. "I'm sure you'd love to stage your own coup and be queen for a day."

She grins with radiating skin. "Nah, when it comes to coups the new guys always end up being as bad as the old ones if not worse," she says in a bubbly light voice.

Ramona appears with her mouth wide open, staggering all over the place. She's dressed untidily, skinny, with long black hair, ripped jeans and a dozen chains and bands around her wrists. She's dressed like a goth and not bad looking if you're into that type of girl. She seems to become aware of her surroundings after viciously shaking her head from left to right. She runs over to the hatch where there's a dispenser of paper towels. She unravels several large pieces and then tears them clumsily. Cackling a deranged laugh, she sprints along the corridor into the recreation room and then to the outside space.

I get up from my chair and move to the right of the massive window in the canteen. She's by the silver birch trees, hanging paper towels on them. When the canteen is nearly empty as most people have finished their meal, she makes her way back into the ward, singing *Bohemian Rhapsody* so loud it's almost deafening.

I turn to Stephanie. "I wonder if there's anything good on TV?"

"I'm more of a reader than a TV junkie," she says. I can't say I read a whole lot, probably nowhere near as much as her but I guess I'll pass myself off as a bookworm.

"What's the last thing you read?"

"*The Communist Manifesto* for school." So, she's definitely a leftie. Well, so is everybody our age. I'll play along because this girl's not only hot but it looks like she's smart too. I might be out of my depth here.

"So, you're a socialist then?" I ask.

Her eyes narrow and she folds her arms. "Isn't everyone with half a heart?" Okay, I've hit a nerve. Regroup, Niall. Regroup.

"Yeah, but you're not one of those dirty commies? Those

MANIC

guys had their day."

Her eyes go cold and hard as her face reddens. "I'm not. But there's still something to be said for the communist ideal on a small scale. There's the potential of a commune working as a household or small farm. Just so long as it's not run by Joseph Stalin."

A commune? My dad's farm would make an excellent commune if only I was in line to inherit and not Conor. I could always work my ass off in the hope of inheriting some of it. Then Stephanie and I could have our commune.

"Anyway," I say. "I was scrolling through the different streaming services on the hospital's TV the other night, and I found a Spiffy Jenkins' stand up. We could watch him."

"Spiffy Jenkins? I love him. He's hilarious." Great, now we've found common ground.

"I'll have a look and see if Martin and Colin will let us watch it. I can't see why not."

I go into the living room and Martin is at the far end of the room, looking slightly dazed. Colin is sitting on the sofa closest to the TV, slouched so low that he's close to falling off it. He grips the remote control in his hand as he glares at me.

"Fancy watching Spiffy Jenkins?"

"You're wasting your time with him. He's not even funny. I mean that name Spiffy. Is that some kind of stage name or something?"

I nod.

"That's fine for musicians, actors and pen names for writers but comedians should have nothing to hide. And Spiffy always dresses in an untidy manner. Is that supposed to be ironic?"

I resist the temptation to highlight to Colin that irony is a form of humour and the ironic thing is, that despite the fact he thinks Spiffy is unfunny (but certainly not without trying), it doesn't occur to him I find Colin's general demeanour and boorish sensibilities hilarious and he's not conscious or even trying. At least not as much as Spiffy.

Stephanie enters the room and Colin sits up.

"Hey, we wanted to watch Spiffy Jenkins if that's alright," she says.

MARK BROWNLEE

"Sure. I love him," Colin says.

Liar. I just don't have the courage to say.

We're halfway through the show and it's probably only right to show Stephanie how fake Colin really is.

"Colin, do you know where Spiffy's from?"

"Berkshire, but he's based in London."

He knew. Stephanie turns and smiles at him in a way that makes me uncomfortable. Does she like Colin more than me?

She holds her grin, staring at Colin who smiles back at her.

"You know your stuff, brainy boy."

Brainy boy? Is she flirting with him? She is.

"He's hilarious," Colin cuts in with a fake laugh.

You are lying through your teeth. Hilarious? We've reached the forty-fifth minute mark and you've hardly laughed at all. I hope Stephanie sees you for who you are.

I've had enough of this. I leave the living room and head towards my room. I pass the art room where a short man with a receding hairline is leaving with a stereo. He turns to me.

"Hi, I'm Jim, the occupational therapist on this ward. Are you interested in doing a relaxation session? There are a few patients waiting in the family room. I just had to run back to get the stereo. Can't believe I forgot it. I've a memory like a sieve."

"Okay," I reply.

We make our way to the canteen area, where Jim sees Colin and Stephanie and gets them to come along too. Once we reach the room at the end of the corridor, we enter and take our seats. The other patients present are Ramona, Colin, Christopher and Stephanie. Jim plugs the stereo into the socket next to where he is sitting and explains what to expect from the session.

He asks everyone to sit comfortably and close their eyes. He has probably played this session hundreds of times before, giving him an opportunity to catch up on paperwork. He silently gestures to me to close my eyes and follow the instructions from the audio. I comply.

I listen to a woman tell us to imagine we are on a desert island, *"a place of peace and serenity."* Then we are to believe

MANIC

ourselves in front of a warm fire with the sound effects aiding our imagination by providing a crackling noise. The woman on the audio asks us to think of one thing that worries or annoys us and then to imagine it as a piece of wood that we put into the fire. We are to believe that our worry will disintegrate in the fire. We are to consider the fire consuming it, providing heat that represents how we have now overcome that worry. Then there are waves as we imagine ourselves lying on a beach. We are to clear our minds of any lingering fears and concerns and focus on the crash of waves and fizz of foam as it sweeps ashore and spreads across the sand. We imagine the gritty sand sticking to our bodies and our wet hair.

I open my eyes. Everybody else is engrossed in the session. Jim is preoccupied with paperwork and hasn't yet noticed that I'm no longer taking part in the activity. I stare at Stephanie. I need to do something to impress her. There is a weight in my chest as I long to hear Stephanie compliment me with her warm voice for something I've done. But it's harder than it sounds. I mean, I bought her that painting which I thought was a dead cert in impressing her. Come on, Niall, think.

I place my hand into my pocket and pull out some change. I have six pound coins, a two-pound coin and a host of silver and copper. I hunker myself on the floor at which point Jim notices I'm no longer doing the activity. When he catches my eye, he shakes his head silently while trying not to distract the others. It doesn't stop me. I bend my body forward and place some of the coins on the floor. I make the shape of a sickle out of the coins. I wait patiently for the audio to finish before standing up and turning to Stephanie.

"You can all help yourselves with my money."

Then I leave the room while everyone's eyes widen and jaws fall open. I look at Stephanie and she's smiling. Yes, jackpot. Heat burns throughout my body as my heart races and drums in my chest. My thoughts scatter all over the place. I'm literally too excited to think but her smile is the only thing constant that makes me conclude that this girl likes me.

Later, standing in the canteen area, I catch Stephanie's

attention.

"Niall, what was that all about in the relaxation session?"

Her question makes me frown. Did I misread her smile? Maybe she doesn't like me? I mean, there are plenty of people I have smiled at and it had nothing to do with me having a desire to hook up with them.

I clear my throat. "We talked about coups and I thought that was a matter of selfishly taking something. We need to be captivated by acts of giving."

"Yeah, but let's not get carried away. Jim didn't actually allow anybody to take your money. So, you'll have to think of a more appropriate act of kindness."

"He might think what I did was part of my illness."

"Nooo? You think?" she says sarcastically.

Did she smile at me because she thinks I'm the comedic idiot? Ah, no. She thinks I'm funny, like the class clown funny not wise guy funny. No. No.

"You're cute," she says, holding a wide grin.

So, I'm cute. Not sure what to think of that. Silence. It's not awkward though. Weird that. I don't usually like silences. Stephanie, she's … she's staring at me, her pupils dilating. This. Is. Awesome. Warmth spreads from my groin outwards. Can anybody else hear my heart hammering?

Oh, but this is it – she's moving closer. Her eyes are shut and her lips are parted. It's really happening.

We're only inches apart, closer, maybe a few centimetres, when Ramona barges between us, flapping her arms and singing *Surfin' Bird* by The Trashmen. Stephanie recoils and clutches her elbows, her eyes darting round the room. Smooths down her skirt. Oh no, no, no, no. How could this have gone so badly wrong?

"I got to go," she says as she turns and runs out of the room.

"Stephanie, wait."

But it's too late. She's gone. How did I miss out on that kiss?

I'm still asking myself that question when Martin appears out of nowhere.

"Hey, Niall. You alright?"

MANIC

It's a fair question, I guess. I'm gazing into the space where Stephanie was standing, playing out fantasies in my head. What would have happened if Ramona hadn't messed things up? What might it have led to later?

I close my eyes. "I think I might be in love."

Ah, I wasn't meant to say that out loud. Now Martin's going to make fun of me.

He cackles. "You sure you haven't just got the wrong 'l' word, mate?"

I crinkle my brow. "What do you mean?"

"It might just be lust, love's dirty cousin. After all, you've only just met the girl. Then again, what do I know about girls."

The warmth in my groin disappears but my heart still pounds. "Well, there is something there even if it ain't love. And do you want to know the amazing thing about it all, mate?"

Martin laughs. "What?"

"I   think   she   feels   the   same   way."

5

WRATH

Friday 20th December

That night I wake up not knowing what time it is. I get out of bed and feel the cold of the floor on my bare feet. I go up to the living room to watch some TV. Before I get there, I'm met by Christine at the staff base.

"What are you doing up so early? It's three o'clock in the morning. Get back to bed and go to sleep."

If I go back to bed, I won't sleep so I remain standing outside the staff base to be scolded by her. In the end, I comply and go back to my room and lie on the bed without sleeping. After a while, I get up and go up to the staff base again.

I knock on the door and Christine turns around from the desk and opens it. She allows me to go to the living room and make myself comfortable on the seat closest to the TV. I switch

MANIC

it on and go through some of the channels before deciding to watch the news. Ramona makes her way along the corridor, enters, and takes a seat opposite me.

So, what's Ramona's story? Before I can think, she asks me a question.

"Are you after any fit-looking birds on the ward?"

I wonder why she asks. Does she assume I'm interested in her? I like Stephanie but I don't tell her. "Why do you ask?"

She laughs. "Because this place is the perfect place for finding the one."

Is she flirting with me? I honestly can't tell.

As we speak, a news story on the DeLorean DMC-12 car is airing on the TV. She turns to me and points to the screen.

"You see that car there?"

I nod.

"We built that."

I shake my head. I've only just met Ramona and have no recollection of us ever personally building a DeLorean car. However, my confusion disappears when she clarifies.

"The DeLorean was built here in the 70s but the company went bust in the 80s. It's a product we can be proud of."

Oh, right. We as people living in the north can say we built the DeLorean car. I didn't know that.

I grin. "Aye, that and the Titanic."

She cackles. "Of course, the Irish have always been masterminds of failure. Later, Skater."

Later Skater? I don't even have a skateboard. Okay, she definitely fancies me. But the feeling isn't mutual. I mean, don't get me wrong, she's a fit goth and I know we're both in a mental hospital but what I know of her so far is that she's proper crazy. I better keep an eye on her though. She and other patients gather in the canteen.

After breakfast, Jim comes to me.

"Fancy doing some artwork with us this morning?"

I'm not really sure whether I want to do all that kiddish arts and crafts stuff I did at primary school. Then again, there probably isn't a lot to do in this place so I might give it a go for now.

"Okay," I say with some hesitation.

I ask Ramona if she wants to join.

"Sure, but first I'm going to light up a fag. Laters."

I go to the art room with Jim and others are already seated. I only know Stephanie, Colin and Christopher. I sit with my back to the window. What initially catches my eye is the artwork on the cupboards, each piece created with varying skill. The bench below has paper, pencils, brushes, bits of clay and paint tiles and containers.

"Okay, everybody. We are going to talk about things that keep us well and prevent us from relapsing into worry, anxiety or depression. Now, what I want you to think of are things or activities that you find will help you keep calm and relaxed. So, Colin, what do you do to help yourself relax?"

"Well, over the past months I've begun to practise mindfulness as well as relaxation."

I frown at what Colin said. I was never, ever into mindfulness but I know my sister really is.

"Good," Jim replies. "We'll hopefully do a relaxation session again sometime for anybody who is interested. Now, Christopher, what about you? What helps you relax?"

"I like to walk my dog Buster around the park. I find it helps clear my mind."

"Lovely. Stephanie, what do you do to relax?"

"I find the thing that helps me relax the most is listening to music."

Hey, she likes music; so do I. I wonder if we have a similar taste so I ask her.

"Ed Sheeran," is her reply.

"Ed Sheeran? What do you listen to him for?" I ask. I notice Jim frowns at the fact I've butted in.

Stephanie's eyes narrow. "Because he's such a talented artist who doesn't only sing but also writes some of the most beautiful lyrics."

Okay, I've stepped on her toe here. But I really don't know why people go mad for him. Granted, he has some amazing songs but then some terrible ones that are still insanely successful.

I clear my throat. "Maybe he's talented and well-received,

but sometimes he's just not my cup of tea."

"Who do you like?"

I'm no musical snob, but when it comes to pop music, I prefer female artists. "Oh, you know, Olivia Rodrigo and Duo Lipa."

"You're a typical guy favouring female artists because of their appearance rather than their singing or song-writing ability." Okay, maybe looks do play a part, but sex sells. Everybody knows that, of course, but I don't say this. If I'm really after this girl, it's best I don't contradict her too much, at least not initially.

"We're getting carried away," Jim intervenes. "Niall, what do you do to help yourself relax?"

"I also like to listen to music," I say, turning to Stephanie who has her arms folded. "Usually, the people I've already mentioned but I find if I run while listening to music, I get a real high and it helps me cope better with stress."

"Excellent. You've all got great methods of keeping your mind in a healthy state. I'm now going to give you the opportunity to carry on with your other projects."

Christopher does some finger painting. Colin assembles a metal car. He finds it difficult as the box does not contain any explicit instructions but he attempts to construct the vehicle as best he can by using the picture on the box. Stephanie is moulding something out of clay – not sure what though. I fidget as I scan everybody else. Jim moves over to me.

"So, Niall, is there anything you would like to do?"

I'm not sure. I don't mind drawing or writing poetry but I'm not any good at it. I don't like people knowing I write poetry but then again, sometimes I think I write some nice gems. I'm a bit of a perfectionist. I could try drawing or writing something, but what?

"How about you create something about your emotions?" he asks

I laugh. "A bit airy-fairy."

"It doesn't have to be. Is there a day that sticks out for you, whether it's positive or negative?"

Yeah. The day I came in here and the manic episode I had before then at home. The mind looks back to that event when all the adrenaline shot through my body, the heart palpitations and the elevated blood pressure. I think back and I write about what happened in the form of a poem:

Wrath

I knew the nukes were coming.
Edwards was going to kill me
they were going to swoop in.

I provoked the Almighty
by shouting all kinds of curses.
But he did not respond.

I was angry with Edwards
that he would nuke my home
and all my family in it.

In my great wrath, I was unsure
where I would finally go
whether it be Heaven or Hell.

My hour had finally come
death came closer as time passed
I was soon to be no more.

But thankfully nothing happened
so, I thanked my loving suviour
for choosing to spare me.

In him, I now put my trust
for he has truly saved me
from death's dark clutches.

I give my life to the LORD
and desire to serve him
in everything, I say and do.

I'm proud of what I have created, so much that I show it

MANIC

to Stephanie, who I am sure will compliment my genius. She rubs off all the loose clay from her hands before taking the page. She leaves a smudge of clay on the bottom corner with her thumb and index finger, then silently reads it. I gulp. Is she going to rip to complete shreds? No, it's a great poem; she won't.

"I know this means a lot to you but do you want my honest opinion?"

Usually when people say something like that it means they're about to say something harsh. But who made her the expert on poetry?

She hands the poem in my direction. "I got an A* in GCSE English Literature. I know a thing or two about poetry," she says, trying to fill our awkward silence

My limbs shake ever so slightly. Is she going to tear it apart? There is only one way to find out. "Okay, shoot," I say.

"I think it needs a bit of work. It lacks any rhyme, imagery, similes or metaphors. You've created some sort of metre as each line is roughly seven syllables but this isn't always consistent, and the whole point of a metre is to create rhythm, something this poem greatly lacks. It also lacks any real vividness of feeling you must have felt from your traumatic experience. There is a build-up of tension at the start and the middle in this poem then it just drops dead with the words, 'But thankfully nothing happened'. I hope I haven't hurt you."

Hurt? That's exactly how I feel. I poured my heart and soul into that poem and then she, somebody I barely know, has the cheek to rip it apart. Surely, she must know what it means to me. I feel a hardness in my gut but conjure up the strength to say, "It's okay. I don't know as much about poetry as you do. Do you write any poetry yourself?"

She smiles as she moulds the clay again. "I do, but my poems are very personal. I don't like sharing them. I could recommend some famous poets to help you get better at it."

I don't need to read any famous poets. Poetry for me isn't all about literary merit, Stephanie. It's about expressing the rawness of one's emotions. It's not about becoming a clone of some famous poet. If I did that, I would no longer be my true authentic self. But I don't tell her this.

MARK BROWNLEE

"I'd appreciate that," I say.

"You should start with poets like Billy Collins as he's easy to get into."

I nod but have no intention of reading Mr Billy Collins. My poem is good enough without any sort of edit. Why can't she see that?

"Stick at it. You can only get better," she says.

"Let's have a look at your poem, Niall," Jim says, clearly eavesdropping on our conversation.

"Stephanie says it's not very good."

"No, I didn't. I said it needs a bit of work," she says, with a rigid body posture and rising colour in her cheeks. She might as well have said it wasn't good because I feel as if she did.

"Poetry's a very personal thing," Jim says. "Give it over."

I know it is. I wish Stephanie thought the same way rather than giving a vicious criticism of something so close to me. Jim's got to be more empathetic so I hand him the page.

He slowly reads it to himself. "It's good, Niall. You're honest about emotions and your circumstances, and that's what I like the most about your poem."

Thank you. Now why didn't Stephanie say the same?

"Have you thought about drawing something that relates to this poem and the events surrounding it?" Jim adds.

"Not really."

"How about you draw a face expressing your thoughts and emotions."

I frown. I was psychotic at the time. I sit for several minutes, looking around, thinking the exercise is pointless. But everybody else is so quiet and getting on with their different projects so, eventually, I put pencil to paper.

I think of something along the lines of Edvard Munch's *Scream* painting. As I begin to create the drawing, it starts to take shape. Rather than create a sunset scene in Munch's work, I focus solely on the head. I create an abstract representation of the head with curved lines, a fat nose and slanted eyes. The mouth is open from top to bottom to convey the continued shouting I produced throughout my episode. In addition to all this, I become even more abstract by drawing flames in the brain area of the head around a body tied to a pole. They

MANIC

represent the fire left by the nuclear strike I was convinced was going to take place that day. They also express the flames of Hell I thought my body and soul were destined to quench.

Once I've finished, I show it to Stephanie, excitedly. "What do you think?"

"It's alright."

I roll my eyes.

"Let's not get ahead of ourselves," she adds.

Get ahead of ourselves? Speak for yourself, Mrs I got at A* in my English Literature, and now thinks she's God's gift to humanity.

Jim walks over to both of us. "I want you both to define positive human values in your own words. If I'm happy enough with your work, I'll display it on the foyer wall. I'll give you eight values to work on: peace, hope, life, courage, inspiration, recovery, faith and confidence."

"Let's start with peace," I say.

"Cool," Stephanie says. "I suppose you could say, 'Men want war at times ...'"

I cut in. "Hang on, men want war at times? Don't you think that's a tad sexist?" I know I've held back from confronting Stephanie but I think she's out of line with men always starting wars.

"It's a common fact that men are the ones who start wars."

"Maybe in the past, but since we have more women in authority, they must take the brunt of the blame."

Stephanie's jaw drops. "You're such a guy."

"What's that supposed to mean?" I say through gritted teeth.

"You're afraid of any minor threat to the patriarchy. The majority of senior positions within our society are still held by men." Oh, come on. There are numerous female politicians and leaders in the business world today. I mean, you can even have women as soldiers.

"Whatever," I say.

She takes a deep breath then sighs. "What about courage?" she asks.

"How about, *'There is no courage without fear'*?"

"I like it," she says. "Even though it's a quote from a Tom Cruise movie."

There she goes again, shooting me down when I'm flying high or at least trying to.

"Yeah, but what a movie. *Edge of Tomorrow* is one of my favourites of all time. It has such a great premise."

She sneers. "It's an action movie with the same premise as *Groundhog Day*. It's hardly original."

Jim interjects. "You two are like a married couple, like Abba." No, we aren't married and even if we were, that wouldn't be a great reference since the creative process destroyed both couples' marriages.

After we finish, Jim takes what we have written and says he will be putting it up in the foyer for other patients to see. I go to the canteen and take a seat. A Socrates quote comes to mind which aptly describes all the bickering and arguing with Stephanie this morning. I put the words of the father of European philosophy on my Facebook wall.

"By all means marry. If you get a good wife, you'll be happy. If you get a bad one, you will become a philosopher."

If I ever decided to be stupid enough to even consider marrying Stephanie, I have no doubt that I would pen the greatest philosophical work this world has ever known. No, really, I'm not exaggerating.

I set my phone on the table and sigh. Then turn and see Martin walking up the corridor.

"Well, how's Romeo? Has Juliet been asking for you from her balcony?"

I shake my head and grit my teeth. "I hate her."

Martin frowns. "What? One minute you love her and now you hate her?"

"I wrote a poem in the art room and then she ripped it to shreds," I say with a raised voice.

"I'm sure she didn't mean any harm," Martin says.

I huff.

Then Stephanie walks towards us. "Niall, I was wondering if you would like a coffee with me after lunch?"

I sigh. "I'll think about it."

She leaves us with a lowered head and hunched posture.

MANIC

"Call me crazy," Martin says, "but you two would make a nice couple. So don't think too long on her little date."

My phone vibrates in my pocket and I notice I have a missed call from my dad and a voice message:

"Do you have any idea what you being in hospital is doing to me and your mum? I've enough problems as it is without you making things worse. I get up at 6:30 every morning to milk cows while you're lying in bed feeling sorry for yourself. Nevertheless, your mum wanted me to ring you. You know how hopeless she is with phones. Since you are losing your senses, I highly recommend you read the text which is the bedrock of Western civilization: Plato's Republic. I have no doubt that when you read it, all your mental problems will disappear. I have no disposable copies at present as I cherish the one I have. I know you might be struggling to read at present but you can always listen to books being read to you on your phone. I hope you get well soon. Deus te Benedicat."

Two book recommendations in two days. Dad, please, give me a break.

6

VERITAS

Friday 20th December

'm at the table having lunch with Martin. Patients are murmuring and the cutlery is clinking and scraping against the plates.

"I'm telling you, Niall. You have to go with Stephanie after lunch," he says.

"No. Her head's that far up her ass she has fallen in love with her own farts."

Martin laughs. "Well doesn't everybody love their own fumes? Woh" he says whiffing his hand over his nose.

I laugh. Okay, we all do but I still hate her.

He takes a forkful of food and swallows. "Okay, so she hit a nerve when she criticised your poem but she probably meant nothing by it. She thinks no less of you if she wants to have coffee with you."

MANIC

It's a fair point but I don't want to have coffee with her. I nod slightly. "Maybe."

Martin wiggles his eyebrows; his eyes have a twinkle of mischief. "Look, I can do a little deal with you."

I turn and he's grinning. "Five quid says you'll … *love her* … after having coffee with her."

I frown. "No, I won't," I say as my ribs tighten.

He takes his wallet out and removes a five-pound note. "Look at this bit of dosh with the image of the king himself. Sure, you can't resist the money – and Stephanie, of course."

I say nothing. I did like Stephanie when I first came into the hospital and we nearly kissed. Despite everything that happened this morning, it was something for her to ask me to have a coffee. But should I?

"Come on. There is money to be had."

I sigh. "Alright, I'll go. But only for the money."

I finish my meal and find Stephanie in the lobby area, grinning. The place is marked with pale walls and fluorescent lighting. Slippers whisper over the floor as a heavily sedated patient drags his feet across the hospital.

"Have you recovered from occupational therapy?" she asks with a grin.

I don't know what she means exactly. I know more broadly she's referring to the little argument we had over the values we eventually agreed upon.

"Have a look," she says, pointing to a board on the wall, and there are the values we had discussed. Jim must have liked them and put them on display.

"My personal favourite is our definition of peace," she says.

I say nothing as I read it into myself:
"Men and women want war at times.
They raise their swords for battle
but they should all sheath their weapons
and pick up olive branches instead."
I nod when I finish reading.

"Let's just say we both drew our swords a little this morning. Can we pick up olive branches or, at the very least, sheath our swords," she says, gesturing a sword being

MARK BROWNLEE

sheathed.

I nod slightly but still say nothing.

She cracks a smile. "You're not saying much. Has the cat got your tongue?"

"I suppose you could say that."

"Well, the peace offering I want to give is a coffee and a little game," she says with an upturned face.

Game? My breath briefly stops and there's a tingling in my neck. "What's the game?"

"That's for you to find out. What do you say?" she asks, offering me her hand.

The whole thing is a pile of rubbish, and I'm about to tell her that but then I turn back along the corridor. Martin tries to hide from me by running into a room. Look, I know it's only five quid, but Mum took my wallet and I spent all the cash on that painting she didn't even accept from me. If I go to the cafe, Martin won't be eavesdropping and I can lie to him about whatever happens and get my fiver. Desperate times call for desperate measures. Okay, here goes.

I clutch her hand, and we run along the corridor to the hospital cafe in an instant. My heart races because of the quick pace we're moving at and no, nothing to do with any romantic attraction I might have towards her. I'm not sure I want to be doing this with Stephanie, but here I am. We approach the counter. There's an acrid scent of burned coffee as Stephanie meets the barista's gaze.

"What can I get ya?"

"Latte."

"Americano," I add.

The barista makes Stephanie's order using the frothing machine. The machine grinds coffee beans when she makes my order. The cash machine rings when she gives us our coffee. We cautiously sip our coffees and sit at a table.

"So, what is this little game you want me to play?" I ask, blowing ripples on the top of my drink.

"Have you ever played truth or dare?"

"Ah, don't tell me you got me here to play a stupid game of truth or dare," I say, standing up about to leave, spilling some of the coffee on my hand. I flinch, then try to shake the

MANIC

hot liquid off me. It's really hot.

She raises her hand, gesturing to me to sit. "Niall, I merely asked if you've played it before. I didn't say we were going to play now."

I sit down again. A visitor comes through the main entrance carrying a bunch of flowers. A patient runs along the corridor clutching their head, screaming aloud, and is chased by two nurses. Stephanie and I follow them along the corridor with our eyes.

"To be honest, I never liked playing truth or dare," she says.

That's reassuring. Although I don't say this. I sigh and I turn to Stephanie.

She is smiling. "One half of it, I hate. But there's one half that I love and it's always a good way to break the ice and get to know somebody."

I've no idea where she's going with this, but I'm curious, so I listen in.

"It's the dares I hate. I mean, the dares descend into childhood antics."

Really? I prefer doing any number of dares if it means people don't get to know who the real Niall Alexander is. For some reason, I find myself wanting to play this game to find out what Stephanie's like.

She takes a small sip of her latte. "So, to make this game interesting, I prefer to play the game of truth or lie. When it's each person's turn, they have to tell a truth or lie about themselves, and the other person has to work out what is the truth and what is the lie. What do you think?"

I smile. "Truth without the dare?"

She nods with a smirk. "It's for those of us that are more risk-averse and are also convincing liars."

A young sleeping patient across from us starts to snore. I swallow hard. That's exactly the way I'll turn out if I go on meds. I shake my head and turn to Stephanie.

"Okay. I'm in. You lead the way."

She pensively looks up at the ceiling. "Okay, truth or lie? I have an evil twin called Angelica. Or I have never been outside of the north before."

Hang on. Surely both of those are lies. I mean, I doubt she has an evil twin sister, but then again, maybe she has a twin but she says she's evil to throw me. I mean, it could be argued we're all evil. You know what they say: nobody's perfect. Regarding not being outside the black north, that must be the lie.

"You've never been outside the north is the lie," I say.

She shakes her head.

Hang on, what? A sudden heaviness expands in my core. "Why have you not been outside the north?"

"I don't know. I've never been that adventurous. My friends say I'm a bit of a bookworm. I travel through books. It's fun. I've been to Hogwarts, Narnia and Middle Earth without ever leaving my bedroom."

It's sad she has missed out on seeing the world. "Is there anywhere you would like to see?" I ask.

"Nowhere is as safe and homely as my books. My mum is a real introvert. I guess I take after her. We don't like anything better than sitting around in silence reading books."

"Come on. You need to be more adventurous." I feel sorry this girl hasn't seen the world.

Laughter sounds from the television, which is bolted into the corner of the room, as it beams out daytime TV. There is a squelch of rubber gloves as the cleaner disposes of them into a metal bin.

"Okay, now it's your turn: truth and lie."

My mind races, trying to find ideas. The silence between us and Stephanie's gaze makes me feel exposed and judged. After rubbing my chin for several moments and rolling my eyes pensively, I know what my truth and lie is.

"I've been to Rome. I've read all of James Joyce's *Ulysses*."

I decide on giving her an easy one to start with but the more time she takes to consider my statements the more I question whether it's easy.

"Name two characters from Ulysses?" she asks.

Does she actually think I've read all of Ulysses? I mean, that book's huge and so boring. I've read bits and pieces, so I know the main characters.

"Leopold Bloom and Stephen Dedalus."

MANIC

She scratches the top of her long ginger hair which she has tied back into a ponytail.

"I guess the visit to Rome is the lie."

"Wrong," I cackle.

"You've been to Rome," she gasps. "What was it like?"

"I could tell you all about it but you sort of have to be there to believe it," I laugh and slap my thigh.

She smiles.

"No, really. Yes, you can read stuff in books, you can look through travel guides, but you'll never know what a place is like unless you're there. Books are mere shadows of real things. You need to get out there and live a little, Stephanie."

She smiles. "Yes, I'd love to but unfortunately, I'm stuck in a psychiatric hospital right now with you."

I'm not sure if she's complimenting or insulting me.

"Your turn."

"Okay. I once shoplifted. I once won a spelling competition."

She's not just a self-confessed bookworm, she's also an open book. There's no way she's ever shoplifted in her life. Everything I know of her so far is telling me that she won a spelling competition. But maybe that's what she wants me to think. Is it too obvious to be true? I think not.

"It's a lie that you once shoplifted."

"Wrong," she yells, then smiles. "Well, I never did it deliberately. I was changing in a charity shop and kept on an item of clothing without knowing. I only realised when I got home that night."

"That's not shoplifting because you didn't do it on purpose."

"Did I say I did it on purpose?" she says with a raised eyebrow. "So, it's still shoplifting."

"If you think what you did is shoplifting, you've lived a very, very sheltered life."

She smiles. "Your turn."

Once again, I ponder what to say but I smile when I decide on two statements. I want to show her the importance of living life on the edge.

"I once got arrested. I recently ran outside my house

naked."

A long pause ensues as she frowns and rubs her chin. Have I totally stumped her?

Eventually, she turns to me. "Why did you run outside your house naked."

"It felt like a good idea at the time," I say, trying my best to stifle a laugh but with little success as there's a lightness in my limbs and an overall feeling of weightlessness. I'm not sure which statement I'm implying is true with my laughter. To be honest, I don't care.

"What were you arrested for?"

I smile, holding in a laugh as heat goes through my chest and my hands tingle. "For running around outside my house naked."

"But that's ... aw shut up."

Then there are sudden pains in my stomach as I laugh until it hurts while Stephanie hits me on the bicep.

I laugh like I've just got laughing gas from the dentist.

"You need to grow up."

"Grow up? You're the one that still plays a lame, immature version of truth or dare."

If I laugh anymore, I'm probably going to get the hiccups.

"So, both statements are either true or false. Which is it?"

I regain my composure. "The truth is Stephanie, I lie about the truth."

She frowns and tilts her head to one side. "What is that supposed to mean?"

"Think about It then get back to me. Your turn."

"Okay, to prove that I'm neither lame nor immature, like my contestant who doesn't follow the rules, I will ask which statement is true of me and which one is the lie. I like Niall. I like Colin."

I stop laughing. "What do you mean by 'like'?"

She smiles. "Well, since you broke the rules of the last round, I can bend them by not explaining what I mean by 'like'. Why not have an air of mystery?"

Does it matter to me who Stephanie likes? After all, I'm not sure if I like her. But for some reason, I wanted it to be true that she likes me. The idea that she likes Colin over me makes

MANIC

my lungs constrict and brings a painful tightness in my throat.

"You like me."

"Yes and no," she replies.

"What's that supposed to mean?"

She smiles, and I gaze into her gorgeous blue eyes. Right now, there's a twinkle in them, and there's a fluttering in my stomach.

"The truth is, Niall, I lie about the truth." She bursts into laughter.

Hey, that's my line. Other patients and staff are congregating at the counter of the café, ordering drinks and helping themselves to tray bakes.

I have to say I'm surprised at how intelligent Stephanie is. I'm lightheaded and there's an expanding feeling in my chest. I swallow to relieve the dryness from my mouth, which is hanging open in awe.

She laughs at me so I close my mouth. I probably look like a right prat.

"Now, it's your turn. Only this time we follow the rules, okay?"

I nod. I think for several moments.

"You ready?"

"Yes."

"Shoot."

"I love Stephanie O'Reilly. I love Ramona Reynolds."

She laughs. "Love is a very strong word to use to refer to two people you've only just met."

"Hey, you can interpret love whatever way you want."

"I will. But I'm interested in the person who declares one of these statements true.

What does he think love is?"

"Don't the Greeks have four meanings for it?"

"Yes, but he isn't Greek, and he's sitting right in front of me so he can explain which Greek meaning he means."

"I can show it."

"How?" she asks with mischievous lips that are just asking to be kissed.

I close my eyes, tilt my head to the right and clench my lips. They're met by Stephanie's. I place my hand on the back of her neck. When we part, I open my eyes to those beautiful irises, a wondrous sea of blue.

"I guess I got a kiss without beating you at table tennis."

"That was just a sample. To get the full works, you're still going to have to beat me at table tennis. I doubt that'll ever happen."

She taps me on the thigh and then leaves. I stare into space for a time until a voice speaks behind me.

"No fiver for you, mate."

I turn around. It's Martin. Fiver? My thoughts are fixed on the kiss. Yes, the fiver. But the kiss. Priceless.

7

THE EPISODE

Friday 20th December

'm with **Stephanie and Martin** in the family room, getting into the festive spirit by opening a box of Christmas crackers we've found. The jokes inside are terrible.

"What did the sea say to Santa?" Martin asks. Stephanie is deep in thought with anticipation in her eyes.

She shakes her head. "Don't know."

Martin smiles. "Nothing. It just waved."

She laughs while I say nothing, there are more important matters that have overcome me. Will President Edwards ever meet me in person? Should I phone the White House to achieve this? What about the Russians? I feel my jaw fall open. Yes, it's the Russians who are the real threat now. They're going to nuke the hospital.

MARK BROWNLEE

Quick, Niall. You must stop this. Something tells me if I flush the toilet in my en suite room, it will do something. Yes, it will stop imminent nuclear destruction. A voice confirms my suspicions. *Niall, get up from the table, go to your room and flush the toilet.* It sounds simple, even harmless. *Niall,* the voice persists, *go to the bathroom. Go on.*

I walk along the hallway to my room. I enter the bathroom and lock the door behind me. *That's it, Niall. You've made it here, now sit on the toilet.* I lift the seat and sit down.

I pause. This is the moment of truth. I'm not quite sure what will happen next. Will the world be nuked at the very moment I flush? Or will the flush bring about a chain of events that will make nuclear destruction less likely? There is only one way to find out.

I'm reluctant to follow through with the action, still intrigued about what will happen if I flush. *Niall, flush it. I promise you, you won't regret it.* Obedience to the voice seems to be the best course of action.

My shaky hand is on the handle as the rest of my body moves back. I close my eyes and push down. The flow of water descends from the rim of the bowl to its bottom. A roar follows the tap of dripping water as the tank refills itself. I open my eyes. Nothing. I let out a sigh.

At the sink, I freshen up in the mirror in front of me. As I stare at the image of myself, the song, *The Final Countdown* by Europa, roars from another patient's room. Is that the final countdown to the end of the world? There is a churning in my stomach and my insides are quivering. I imagine myself on stage performing the song to a packed-out stadium of thousands. Until the song is butchered by my consciousness entering the singer's body, and my talentless self receives all the shouts and jeers from a disapproving crowd.

I close my eyes and see myself dancing with Stephanie. If I'm about to die, I want to think of things I like. She's on the floor and then I fall on top of her. I pull her up by the arm, and waltz with her, swaggering around an extravagantly decorated ballroom.

I open my eyes and there, in front of the mirror, I say, "You are the one, Stephanie. The one for me, my angel." I place

MANIC

my forehead on the mirror and turn it from side to side. My eyes lock on their reflection.

Then there's a knock on the door. "Are you alright, Niall?" It's her. I open the door and grab her by the palms and waltz with Stephanie along the hallway.

"One, two, three, one two, three, one, two, three, one, two, three," I say as we dance together, her with more fluid movements without any hesitation. She laughs and her eyes sparkle and shine. But she quickly leaves when she realises she has to talk to one of the nurses. I go back into my room alone.

I'm silent as I close my eyes again and imagine Stephanie, with her ginger hair, naked. Her neck arched, her ginger hair perfectly straight, and her pale milky skin. Her pupils sharpened by her immense intellect. I sing *Stephanie Says* by The Velvet Underground.

I hear a laugh outside my room and see Stephanie through the door window. Then I sing *The Star-Spangled Banner* in the hope that the Americans might do something about the nuclear threat. This makes her frown. Then it hits me – President Edwards, my hero, my idol, is dead, killed in a decapitation manoeuvre. Now, with America leaderless, the Russians are able to carry out a nuclear strike. They could kill me by carrying out a military strike against me. Perhaps they'll use conventional forces like drones to take me out. Yet what if they're so enraged that they would still consider the nuclear option?

I leap up from my bed and run, my arms flailing erratically. Along the hallway, back into the family room where Martin is sitting pulling crackers apart.

"The whole hospital is about to be destroyed," I shout. "I can't believe you're going to kill everybody, you Russians. These are all good people; why will you let them all die? Curse you! Curse you!" Martin's eyes widen. He has a slack mouth and he is suddenly still. There's a pressure in my chest as I forget to breathe and an uncontrollable shudder sweeps through my entire body. I feel my bottom lip shake uncontrollably and the rims of my eyelids fix open. I'm going to die. The whole world is about to come to an end. The Russians are about to send all their viable nuclear armaments to pulverise me and every atom in a one-hundred-mile radius of the hospital. Their combined destructive power will form a chasm that will open the very depths of the earth's core and spill its molten contents into dark, lifeless, space. A beautiful picture, only enjoyed by the Almighty.

I want to die before the nuclear missiles reach their mark. "Blessed Mary, the Virgin Mary, Mary the mother of God, Mary!" I roar.

I shut my eyes so the darkness of my intentional blindness will lead me to a happy afterlife. But light breaks through the cracks of my eyelids. The Mother of God must be watching from above. If only she will persuade the Almighty to intervene on my behalf. The bright lights of Heaven are where I want to be.

Time drags on and my death is drawing near. There is a burn of vomit in the back of my throat and I feel a sudden drop of temperature in my body. Will I go to Heaven, Purgatory or Hell? Perhaps the answer can be found in my room?

I dash in, grab my Bible and open it to find answers but to no avail. I raise its leather cover above my head and down onto it. Surely this is enough to send me to a happy afterlife in Heaven. It doesn't. There is other literature in my bag. I pull a book from the Divine Comedy box set. Perhaps it might save me or help me reach Heaven. I bang it against my head in the hope that it will take me to paradise. But I'm horrified that the book I've been banging my head with isn't Dante's *Paradiso* but his *Inferno*. I rip the front cover off and throw it into the bin. I cry out to Saint Michael to protect me.

The nukes are now only minutes away from impact. The question now is where will I spend eternity?

Will a Gulag be my insufferable afterlife? Forced to carry out arduous labour with harsh punishments, including torture. Or will an eternity in a darkened cell be my ultimate destination? Stuck in a place where my cries or screams go unheard. My open eyes are blinded by the darkness, where there will be no relief from my eternal hardship. The place will be utterly empty of all objects that I can use to take my life, which will be impossible since the darkened cell will be the tortuous afterlife I will have to suffer forever. My hope of

MANIC

Heaven is now pointless; I'll experience eternity, forever climbing a never-ending rope from the earth to the sun. I throw the books on the bed and head to the canteen where patients are congregating.

"I know this seems above some of you but can one of you get me a rope and throw it around the sun so that I can climb up to it." My speech is pressurised as I hyperventilate with my jaw clenching and my teeth gritting. I must look like a fool but I don't care. Something has to be done and fast.

The sun will be a better place to be than a nuked earth.

Everyone's silent.

Then the Russian President speaks to me. *You are a good-for-nothing rat, and you will spend eternity not in Heaven or Hell, but as a rat entombed in a never-ending drainpipe, crawling for eternity through its black faeces that will soil your vermin hide. You will be smothered to the degree that you'll struggle to move. Utter darkness will be your friend, with your eyeballs as useful as a pair of emasculated testicles. You want to die? Do you want relief? You want somebody here to shoot you with a gun? You'll have to beg for the bullet. You'll have to suck on it until you choke. Beg for it. Beg for the bullet.*

"I'll suck the bullet," I cry. "I'll suck the bullet!" I scream. "Please, give me the bullet," I say in deep distress, hoping one of those present might kill me. Poetic justice for all the wrong I had done to people over the years. I experience a numbness and a heart that aches. There's a thickening in my throat as if my heartbeat is there. Would the patron saint of the poor, St Francis, come in now and put me out of my misery by shooting me dead?

"Get Francis. Come on, Francis. I'll suck the bullet. Come on, Francis, shoot me. I deserve it."

I'm on the floor and everyone around me has a familiar on their shoulder, a symbol representing their soul and character. Each is an animal or mythical creature. Who is my familiar? I don't know. Do I even have a soul? I desperately cry out in the hope of gaining one. "Mouse, rat, rat, mouse, lizard, dragon, lizard, dragon, lizard, dragon, horse, donkey, mule, horse, donkey, mule, cat, cat, cat, cat, cat, crab, turtle."

Then Stephanie, the nurse Christine and an old, retired

banking nurse enter the room and peer down at me. I gaze at them and receive a smile and nod, probably trying to calm me down and reassure me that everything is okay.

I'm perplexed by their faces.

I consider the beauty of Christine's complexion. Her face is that of the elven queen, Galadriel, staring back at me, the ethereal wisdom in her sharp blue eyes cushioned by her delicate cheeks. Her face is surrounded by the long curls of bleach-blonde hair. Stephanie has an appearance comparable to the fiery hair and pale countenance of the goddess Venus. Then the face of the older nurse, her dark hair and wrinkled face, leads me to believe she is the very Mother of God.

The three persons of the Trinity – Galadriel, Venus and Mary – stare at me from their elevated position with their familiars – a Griffin, a Phoenix, and a Chimera. Their presence brings me to hope in redemption. The head of Christine moves closer to me, but why? I lash out and growl at her. I don't want compassion from anybody, for I lie condemned. Two male nurses quickly come to both sides of me.

Stephanie stares at me and I gaze back but my eyes grow wet and my vision goes blurry.

"Stephanie ... I ... ah."

She draws closer. I feel like I've got a bullfrog stuck in my throat. I cough several times and I lift my head and struggle to get my words out but only manage to utter gibberish. Then I bang the back of my head against the floor and blackout.

8

AFTERMATH

Saturday 21ˢᵗ December

You certainly are full of surprises," Stephanie says, standing at my bedside.

"Where am I?" I ask, looking around the room. What about the Russians and the nukes? And what about President Edwards? My heart races so much that there is a pain in my chest. I feel dizzy and there's a weakness in my legs and knees. My stomach is rock hard. I turn away from Stephanie onto my side and let out a yelp.

"Is this real?"

"Yes, Niall. This is real."

I turn to face her on the bed. "But only what you feel is real."

Stephanie frowns.

"Are you real?" I add.

"Of course, I'm real. I exist."

I ponder her words for several seconds. "But you weren't real before I met you."

She smiles but shakes her head. "I existed before you knew me."

"But I didn't know you existed."

She laughs. "Niall, just shut up and don't start giving me all that rubbish about if a tree falls in a wood and is never heard does it make a sound. I didn't intend to get into a philosophical debate, I just wanted to see how you were doing."

Stephanie places a hand on my shoulder. I look up to her big pretty blue eyes. It's very rare for gingers to have blue eyes. I think it's one in a hundred. Stephanie would always stand out in any crowd of a hundred.

"Relax, Niall. They moved you to a more open room on the ward so they can keep a closer eye on you."

"I ..."

"You just got a little carried away but you're fine now."

The room is much larger than my previous one, with hospital equipment stationed in the corner and a nurse is sitting in the doorway. I turn to Stephanie and smile. She reciprocates. There's a lightness in my chest when I gaze at her face. My insides are vibrating and I have a dry mouth. I try to say something but merely stutter out gibberish. She laughs. I hope with me and not at me.

Then her smile turns to a frown. "Look, Niall. There's something really important I need to tell you ..."

Mum and Dad rush into the room. Stephanie stands awkwardly as they enter then quietly leaves, much to my annoyance.

"Niall, are you okay? What happened? We heard there was an incident," Mum says.

"Yeah, Niall. What are you playing at?" Dad asks. Great, here we go again. The great bane of my existence. The Apostle Paul had his thorn in the flesh, his messenger from Satan and all the theologians theologise in their ivory towers about who or what it was. In my case, my thorn is called Daniel Alexander or, as he likes to be called, but certainly doesn't deserve the

MANIC

title, dad.

"Please, Daniel. He has been through a lot," Mum says.

Dad sighs.

"Niall, we talked to the consultant and he told us you haven't been taking your medication and this is why you had another episode," Mum says calmly.

"They're only going to slow me down."

"They're only going to make you sane," Dad grunts.

Mum places her hand on mine. "You need to take them. We're all really worried about you. You need to take them to get better."

Dad huffs. "Son, what's your reason for not taking them?"

"I, ah ..."

"Oh, this'll be good," he says with his arms folded. I was never good enough in Dad's eyes; he always favoured Conor over me. There's the argument that I was an accident because my parents were already happy with a son and daughter. Then I came along and spoiled everything. Mum, of course, always adamantly denies this; Dad denies it but just not as adamantly as Mum.

"Daniel, please. You need to be more considerate," Mum says.

"If I start taking tablets, I'll become a couch potato. You don't want that." Knowing Dad, he probably would. From his point of view, this looks bad to all family, friends and neighbours and you can't forget all his former university colleagues. All the rumours that are no doubt spreading. He's probably more concerned about them than me.

"Niall, what I want you to do is to talk sense. If that means you are taking tablets that will sedate you, I will gladly make you pay that price," he shouts.

His words are like needles in my head but I'm not going to keel over and die just yet.

"You don't give a toss about what I want."

"Niall," Mum says. "We're both concerned about you and we want you to get better. It's in your interests to take your tablets."

My interests? That's rubbish! But I hold my tongue for a moment "No. I will not and you can't force me."

"The staff have the power to force you," Dad barks. Yeah, and if it wasn't them, he'd love to force me to take the medication, and I'd say he'd get a real kick out of it

"No."

Dad frowns. "Well, it'll only be a matter of time before you're forced to make that choice. In many ways you don't have a choice. It'll be made for you. What you're doing is as futile as moving the deckchairs on the Titanic. If you continue to refuse your medication, the staff will have no choice but force you to take them."

I turn to Mum who stares at me and her bottom lip quivers slightly. "We don't want to force anything on you. We are trying to do what's best for you."

Best for me? They have no idea what's best for me. Why can't they just leave me in peace?

There's a hollowness in my chest that feels heavy. I've a slow pulse and my breathing is shallow. "Look, I'm tired. That episode took a lot out of me. I would prefer it if you would leave me alone." Then I turn my back to them on the bed.

"So, that's it. We come all this way and now you tell us to leave. You certainly know how to welcome people," Dad says.

I turn back to face them. "And you certainly know how to counsel someone after a traumatic experience."

"Mind your tongue, son." Mum comes to Dad's side and abates his anger, revealing a bruise on her cheek she has tried to hide with makeup. Dad drunk again. We are his very own punch bags onto which he takes out all his failings in life.

"Let's go, Daniel. We will see you again, Niall. We will keep you in our prayers," Mum says.

Soon Stephanie returns.

"You're probably wondering what my episode was all about," I say.

She grins. "You were unwell, that's all you have to say."

To some, that might be all they have to say and they would be glad that someone only expects that of them. But I feel I have a connection with Stephanie, that I can trust her and explain what was going on in my head. I know it literally was crazy but I feel I can rely on her and I won't scare her away.

"Do you want to know why I had that episode and the one

MANIC

that got me admitted here?"

Stephanie says nothing and I can't tell from her facial expressions if she wants to hear this or not but there is a feeling I need to get it off my chest.

"You've probably heard in the news about Christa Edwards' suicide attempt?" I ask, to which Stephanie nods. "Well," I swallow hard, "I had a crush on her. I wrote a letter to James. Have a listen."

I take out the letter from my pocket.

"'Dear Edwards

Sorry for showing an interest in your daughter. I'd just like to let you know I'm no longer interested. Please don't punish me for what I've done. I know what you Americans are like, so I'm begging you, please. No drones, snipes or A-bombs like Hiroshima and Nagasaki. I like Armagh and I would much prefer it if you didn't turn it into a nuclear wasteland.

Yours Sincerely,

Niall Alexander.'"

Stephanie leans forward. "Niall, please don't take this the wrong way because I think you are a great guy, but have you been taking your medication?"

I laugh. "Are we playing truth or lie?"

"No, I'm serious. That's what I wanted to talk to you about," she replies.

My thoughts freeze and there is a rising of body heat as I'm unsure where she is going with this.

"Why do you ask?"

"Well, you've just had a pretty serious episode."

I pause for a moment, feeling the weight of the question and the impact either word I could say will have on our relationship. I could lie but something tells me she would find out anyway. I decide on telling the truth because I think in the long run it will serve me well.

"No. I haven't been taking my medication."

"No? Why?" she retorts then sighs. "Niall, we all need to take our medication, no matter what illness we have." Her face turns red and she frowns while putting her hands on her hips.

I don't know what to say after angering the girl of my dreams. I'm only ever going to stand a chance of impressing her

MARK BROWNLEE

if I'm smart, quick and with it. She'll have no interest in me if I'm over-sedated. She wants Superman. Niall Alexander must be Superman.

"That's not your concern."

"It's not my concern?" she says with a raised voice. "Niall, there's something seriously wrong with you."

"And I'm being dealt with sufficiently by being in hospital."

"But you're not taking medication."

I can't tell her why I'm not taking it. I don't want her to realise that I'm just a boring, ordinary guy.

"Look, let's just say we were fooling around before. But I need to be honest with you and say I have my own mental health problems. I think at the minute, if I want to be in a relationship with somebody, I need something stable."

Is she for real? "You're ditching me."

"Niall, I'm just not ready to have a relationship with you. I'm sorry."

"What if I took my medication? What if I got better?"

"I don't know. Maybe. But not yet." After those words, she walks off. My heart feels like it's shrinking and my clenching stomach causes a sudden onset of nausea. This can't be happening.

Do I really want to take medication? I need to stay high to get Stephanie in the short term. But should I play the long game and get better and wait for Stephanie to see me stable and well. If I comply now, I know for sure I'll be over-sedated. But they'll be watching me like a vulture and eventually force me to take the medication. It looks like I've got no choice.

That night, I go to the medication room. I pass all the other patients who silently stare at me. I go into the foyer where Christine gestures to me to take a seat by the door of the meds room.

"We'll have your medication ready in a few ticks," she says.

They start to dispense tablets into a polystyrene cup. Christine places the pills on the trolley and pours me some water then calls me.

MANIC

I stand before the trolley and pick up the cup with the tablets in it. Should I do it? Will I become a couch potato and lose any chance of getting Stephanie? I stare at Christine.

"What would happen if you downed all these tablets?"

She smiles. "I'd be knocked out for six. Ha, maybe more than six."

I swirl the tablets in the cup, staring at them. Should I take them? I hesitantly lift the cup to my mouth, down the pills and go to bed, wondering what will the effect be?

There, I check my phone and notice I have a voice message from Dad:

"Why don't you answer your phone? I talked to a former academic colleague the other day about your situation. Remember, Rome is the light. I raised you as a good Catholic and taught you the classics from an early age so you would have a cultured soul. Don't throw that all away and become more barbaric than a Scythian, by not taking your medication. Anyway, I hope you get well soon. Deo volente."

9

CARPE DIEM

Sunday 22ⁿᵈ December

wake up the following day having had a dream about Stephanie, and in case you were wondering, no, it wasn't a wet one. After breakfast, I scribble everything onto some paper before I forget. To my surprise, it ends up being a poem which I call, *Rejected Love,* the last stanza being the sucker-punch of being rejected by Stephanie:

My lips are clenched
but you don't respond
my eyes now open
you're moving away.

It's alright. Hardly a masterpiece, yet it does express how I feel right now. I rip the page from my notebook and put it in

MANIC

my pocket. It means enough that I want to keep it near at hand, yet at the same time, I need to be careful that nobody sees it, especially Stephanie. I place it in my front jean pocket with my phone. I need a shower but somebody knocks on my door before I can have one.

It's Christine. "You've a visitor," she says.

I stroll up to the family room, and see it's my sister, Niamh, standing outside smiling.

"How are you?"

"Fine," I reply, but I've been a lot better. We both sit around a coffee table covered with mental health pamphlets and a box of tissues. The water-cooler dispenser in the corner bubbles as I sit and clutch the arms of my chair so tightly that my knuckles turn white. The smile is still on her face, almost as if it's there to annoy me.

"Have you met anybody nice?"

"I ..."

My phone starts to buzz loudly. I pull it out and look to see who it is. Daniel Alexander.

I turn to Niamh. "It's Dad."

"Answer it," she says with a nod.

"I don't want to." That's putting it mildly.

"Come on. He's only looking to know how you're doing."

I sigh and answer it. "Hello."

"You nee toooo tak yaur tablets," he shouts in an incoherent slur as I pull the speaker away from my ear. Then I hesitantly place it near again. "Dad?"

"Tak yaur tablets, Niall. Tak yaur tablet ..." he says before being cut off.

"I'm taking them," I say angrily, then hang up. "So, Dad's been drinking?" I say, noticing Niamh curiously pick up a piece of paper from the ground.

"What's this? ... Rejected love?"

Hang on, wait. The paper? I put my hands in my pockets and feel my way around for my poem. No, she has my poem, and she's already reading it. I move forward to take it off her but she raises a hand to hold me off while reading as much of it as possible. If she reads a part of it, she might as well read it all. I don't even try to intervene and watch her read the poem to

68

MARK BROWNLEE

herself. When she finishes, she smiles and nods.

"This isn't half-bad. Who's the girl?" she says with a grin.

"Does it matter? She's no longer interested in me."

"Well, I wouldn't give up. It sounds like you really like her. Stay on her radar and be yourself. You never know what'll happen."

"I can't be myself." I mean, that's the reason why Stephanie knows there's something wrong with me.

Niamh's grinning. "No need to call me Sherlock, but I suspect she's here for a reason, just like yourself, and she wants to hide certain things from you. Trust me, be yourself. It might take time, but it'll pay off."

Be myself? I don't know who I really am. "And who is the real Niall Alexander?" I ask.

"He's smart, funny, blunt and forward sometimes but in a good way. Most of all, and maybe it's something to do with your illness, you aren't afraid of doing anything."

Maybe she's right but, sometimes it has led me to do some weird stuff, like when I wanted to become a priest. Thankfully, this poem is some proof that I don't want that now.

Niamh thrusts the poem in my direction. "That bubbly adventurous side of you is the thing that would turn this girl's head."

I frown and rub my chin. Do you know what? I think she's right. From what I know of Stephanie, I could show her new horizons by living on the edge a bit more.

"How's Mum?"

"Yeah, she's ..." Niamh stops mid-sentence. It's a topic nobody really wants to talk about, like edging around spilt milk on the kitchen floor. It's always there and can't be avoided, no matter how hard any of us try.

"Can you tell from her appearance?" I ask.

"She's wearing more makeup than before. I'm surprised that she, being a teacher, hasn't had a pupil, or at the very least a colleague, notice the difference."

"She's a master of hiding it."

Niamh nods. "Dad's drinking more which doesn't help. I only hope and pray she'll have the guts one day to leave him. Something tells me she won't."

MANIC

I nod but say nothing.

"I got to go. It has been great talking to you. And remember, stay on her radar and be yourself."

I walk around the place and find Stephanie sitting beside the hospital entrance near the cafe. One of the benefits we enjoy at present is having unaccompanied access to the outside, not that either one of us has used the privilege yet. Of course, it's based on our current mental health and compliance with the ward rules. There is a low table in front of where Stephanie is sitting covered with glossy magazines but none interest her. She's reading a sizable thick book, and when I squint at the front cover, I discern the words 'poetry anthology'. Nurses and health professionals are going in and out of the entrance.

I sit beside her. She says nothing, turning a page.

"What are you reading?"

"Poetry."

Well, duh. "Specifically?" I add.

"Rudyard Kipling's *If* ."

I'm in luck. I know that poem but so do most so it's hardly going to impress her. Then I remember Niamh's words: be yourself, be adventurous. If there's anything I remember about that poem, that's pretty much what it's advocating.

"Any good?" I ask.

"Not bad from a patriarchal imperialist."

I forgot Stephanie is a feminist. I'm all for feminism if it means I can go out with her. Hang on. I thought I was trying to be myself. Well, I'm not a misogynist. I mean, I don't think so. Niall, you're getting distracted.

"I know he was a staunch imperialist that got him into trouble sometimes. Yet how is he patriarchal?"

"Here, read the last line."

I look as she hands me the book and runs her finger along the bottom of the poem.

"Can women not do all the things mentioned in this piece?"

I clear my throat. "I've no doubt. But this was written in a different time. Plus, maybe he's addressing a particular young

MARK BROWNLEE

person who happens to be a guy rather than to the general population, which would include women."

"Maybe. Still, I'm not a fan of Kipling."

"Do you know what I think when I read this poem?"

Stephanie makes direct eye contact with me for the first time in our conversation. "What?"

"It's a call to take a risk, go on an adventure. In short, to get out there and live."

Stephanie frowns."And what would you suggest, Odysseus?" she says, closing the book and setting it on her lap.

I don't know that literary reference, but I nod and pretend I do. "It's like the phrase from that movie, seize the day or as they say in Latin, carpie your diaper."

Stephanie bursts into a fit of laughter. "It's carpe diem, you moron."

I know, I just wanted to make her laugh. The phone in reception rings and an angry-looking member of the public appears to want to make a complaint.

I bring my gaze back to Stephanie. "Look, I know my episode may have scared you and given you a lot to think about …"

"It didn't scare me."

"It certainly made you ponder about us being an item."

She says nothing as Dr Henson walks past, coughing. There's a rumbling noise as a cleaner pushes her trolley in the other direction.

"I'll put all my cards on the table, no secrets. I have a bipolar disorder," I say, clutching one hand with the other. There's a brief silence but I'm quick to fill it before it gets too awkward. "To some, that has the same effect as saying you've the plague. I …" Wow, this is a lot harder than I thought. I gulp. "All the health professionals I've talked to say it's a mental illness that can be treated well with medications, which I'm now taking. So, there's hope for me."

She sighs. "Look, Niall. Knowing the problems I have, I just can't go out with somebody with a serious mental illness."

Okay, now I need to apply the Socratic method. "Why?"

"I need stability," she says with a raised voice while making fists at her sides.

MANIC

I flinch slightly. "No, you don't."

"How would you know?" she snarls. Her face goes red and one of her eyelids twitches.

"Because your, like everybody else's, primary goal in life, is to live. Gaining stability is secondary to that."

"To live?" Stephanie rolls her eyes. "That's so vague that it doesn't even mean anything."

"It's vague because everybody needs to find out what it means to live."

She frowns and allows her head to move back from me for a moment. "And suppose you're some guru that knows all the answers?"

"No. Like I said, I'm just a guy with a bipolar disorder. Yet you assume that's a weakness." Stephanie raises her eyebrows while I lean towards her. "Could it be a strength?"

She says nothing, so I continue. "If the purpose of life is to live and experience our deepest emotions. I can assure you I've danced with the angels of Heaven and debated with demons of Hell."

She nods slightly.

"When I look at you, I see someone who always plays it safe. You hid in your books, and don't get me wrong, I love reading as much as the next guy, but I often find myself wanting to be the hero of the stories I read."

She smiles awkwardly. "What are you suggesting?"

"Well, let's start with what you're reading. What does Mr Kipling suggest?"

"He's challenging his readers to become the ideal man. So that rules me out," she says, laughing heartily, tilting her head so far back I can see her snow-white teeth. Man, does she whiten them? They're perfect.

"Well, let's start off easy. What does he say here at the end: *fill the unforgiving minute With sixty seconds' worth of distance run.* I'd say we could do that."

Stephanie curls her lip and wrinkles her nose. "Where are we going to do that? We're in a hospital."

"What about outside?"

Stephanie's face turns ashen, which makes me smile. What is she afraid of? Or perhaps a better question: why is she

MARK BROWNLEE

afraid? Whatever the answer, I know one thing, I need to challenge this girl to get her out of her comfort zone, get her to live.

"No, we can't."

"Come on. Never let the shame of the past or fear of the future shape or define you. Be brave; be the real Stephanie O'Reilly."

"She's a real coward," she says, clutching her book.

"Well, you know what they say. It takes a lot of courage to admit you're a coward," I grin. "Come, let's go on a little voyage of self-discovery."

"No, no."

I hear her 'no', but she's smiling at the same time so, she's halfway to being persuaded.

"Come on. I played your game of truth or lie. I'm asking you to play my game of dare. As you can probably guess, there's only one thing we do in it — dares. So, Stephanie O'Reilly, I dare you to take my hand, come out of this hospital and run as fast as our legs allow us, for sixty seconds, in such a way that would make Mr Kipling proud."

Stephanie presses her lips together in a slight grimace as she becomes quieter and less animated. Then she grits her teeth and tilts her head side-to-side.

"I don't know."

That's good enough for me. I grab her hand and pull her up.

"Niall," she says with a laugh that makes me smile. I've got her on board.

We go outside, running, and she's pulling my arm, going at a slower pace. Finally, after running for more than a minute, sprinting, we're in the hospital car park, bent over panting. I tilt my spine back with my hands on my hips, trying to get my breath back. Stephanie is hunched over, breathing heavily. I go over to her side and get her to straighten up. She smiles at me, now more composed.

"Dare number one complete," I say to her, smiling. "Dare number two? Let's get off the hospital premises."

She says nothing, but nods, still slightly out of breath.

This time we're not running, just walking until we're off

MANIC

the hospital grounds, and we eventually find ourselves in Botanic Gardens. We walk along the meandering paths, through the green space, passing dog walkers. There are still fallen leaves in places from autumn. We navigate our way through the winter trees until we're standing in front of the River Lagan. I stare at it with mischief on my mind, something she notices.

"No, wait. You can't be serious."

"Stephanie, my good friend. Would you like to hear what my next dare is?"

"If it has anything to do with the Lagan, I'll pass."

I try to put on a more serious face. "Remember, it's about living."

Her shoulders and torso loosen slightly as the tension in her body seems to ebb. She offers me her hand. This makes my groin tingle slightly. I grab her and hold my breath as we leap into the water together. My entire body is submerged, and for a brief moment, I'm weightless. Then my head bobs up as I tread water.

Stephanie squeals. "It's freezing."

Yeah, I sort of forgot it was winter and that it would be cold. But it doesn't take long for us to get used to it. She skites some water into my face. There's a slight pull of the river current carrying us along.

"So, Stephanie O'Reilly, after successfully completing three dares, I can officially say, now you're livin'."

She tilts her head back and laughs. But behind her something removes my smile: it's Christine, standing on the bank of the stream with other staff members. Busted. But still totally worth it.

10

COUP D'ÉTAT

Sunday 22nd December

tephanie and I are still shivering with towels around us in the family room, waiting to have a dressing down from Christine.

She comes in with her arms folded. "What were you both thinking? A part of the privilege to have unaccompanied leave is to make staff aware of where you are going. Neither of you did this when you left."

"Sorry," Stephanie and I say as apologetically as possible.

Christine's eyes seem to bulge, "And you thought it was a good idea to jump in the Lagan. One of you could have drowned," she finished with a loud sigh. "It's clear that neither of you are allowed any unaccompanied leave until you restore our trust."

Stephanie nods and I say nothing. I mean, her telling us

MANIC

off and a mere slap on this isn't going to scare me from breaking hospital rules.

"Now get out of here before you make me do something I'll later regret," she says.

We both leave with a tense posture, hunched over. Only when we are outside do we release all the tension from our bodies with fits of laughter. Stephanie goes to her room and I go to mine to freshen up then I head to the ping-pong table. I pass the staff base on the way there but stop suddenly as I peer through the window and see a file with Stephanie's name on it. Man, I would do anything to look inside that. A nurse notices I'm staring at the file and removes it from view. I have to get that but how?

I decide there is nothing I can do at present so I go up and play table tennis by myself with one half of the table up vertically, bouncing the ball back and forth. I still want to win Stephanie's 'full works' kiss in table tennis. I get into the rhythm of hitting the backhand off my racket then flipping it around and hitting it with my forehand. I repeat the motion for a while before I get a brainwave. Do I even need the racket? I throw it on the ground and I hit the ball with my bare hands. It proves more difficult than I'd thought. I flail my arms loosely, like one possessed. Jim frowns as he goes through the foyer. I regain my composure and I pick up the bat and carry on as I did before.

Colin passes by, smirking. "I see we have our very own Forrest Gump on the ward."

I ignore him. Yet when Stephanie comes, I turn to her. "Hey, fancy a game?"

She smiles. "Still desperate for that kiss? I'm not really in the mood for table tennis."

"I'll give you a game," Martin says.

I turn to him behind me.

"There you go," she says. "You boys can play against each other," she grins and leaves.

We start playing and I spin the ball with my serve, Martin responds with a lightning reflex that knocks the ball against my table edge. He raises his arm in triumph.

I watch as nurses and patients pass by. Jim tells people

MARK BROWNLEE

that dinner is ready. He frowns at us as we play table tennis.

"What are you two doing here? Go get your dinner." He turns around and goes into the canteen. We glance at each other then go into the canteen area where tonight, everyone is quiet at their tables. There is the rattle of cutlery, and the noisy sipping of soup as Martin and I walk to the hatch. The cook pours two bowls. I snatch one, causing the soup to spill on my wrist. I'm unphased. We both sit with Colin who smiles and greets us.

Everyone is content to slurp the soup. I stare at Stephanie for some time but ensure that she doesn't notice. My breath hitches and briefly stops.

I finish my soup first, despite staring so much, and dash to the hatch to get more. I finish my seconds before many people have even finished their firsts. Once again, I go up to the hatch to get thirds but before I can, Jim forcefully removes the bowl from my hands and places it on the counter.

"I think you've had enough. Sit down."

I feel my eyes widen and I freeze, but Jim persists. "Sit down now." I remain standing. Jim becomes red faced. He grabs me by the arm, pulls me over to my table and forces me onto a seat.

For the rest of the meal, I never say a word nor does anybody else. I sit with my hands on the table, with a glum face until I find something that makes me grin: Jim's keys are lying on the floor. I pick them up and pocket them before he or anybody else sees me.

Everyone else pours their leftovers into the slop bucket and places their dirty cutlery on the trolley. Most patients go back to their rooms without a word, except for Martin and me. We play another game of table tennis. He's quiet so I decide to do the talking.

"Who does that Jim think he is?"

He smiles as we start our rally. "I know." he says nodding as I hit the ball with a backhand, which bounces on his side before he responds.

"He needs to chill out."

"Maybe smoke a little wacky baccy."

I laugh as he slices a shot and the ball bounces off his side

MANIC

of the table. Martin picks it up and is about to serve it back when I pull Jim's keys out of my pocket.

"Those are staff keys," he shouts in astonishment. I smile and put a finger to his lips. Like my big sis said, I'm willing to do almost anything and that is what I am about to do now.

"Martin, my good friend, do you want to be part of a coup?"

"A coup?"

"A coup that will end the tyranny of Jim Ratched."

"You can't be serious."

"I'm deadly serious. When the nurses lock the staff base tonight to give out the medication in the foyer, we'll unlock the doors and take control of the staff base."

"Why?" he asks.

"Have you no imagination? So, we can look at patient files. Knowledge is power. I want to know what they've written about all the other patients, Stephanie in particular. What about you? Wouldn't you like to know what they've written about you in their files?"

It doesn't take him long to realise that he would also be interested in looking at patient's notes but particularly his own.

He nods.

"We'll wait outside the staff base until the evening nurses leave. Then we'll make our move."

But Martin tries to pick holes in my plan. "In the evening, the nurses will have keys to get back in. Plus, if they find us too much to handle, they can always sound the alarm and get more nurses from other wards to assist them."

"Don't worry. I've thought this through. Before we make our way into the staff base and lock it, we'll lift the sofa outside and bring it in. When they try to break in, we'll brace it against the door. It'll hold them off for a while."

"A while?" he says with a frown. "So, you expect this plan to fail even from the beginning?"

"Well, I admit they'll get in eventually but we'll put up a good fight. Don't worry about the consequences. Staff in these places have to take such guff all the time. The worst they'll do is move you to another ward. Act real crazy and you'll be fine."

MARK BROWNLEE

Several hours pass before it's the usual time for the patients to receive their medication. Christine is working in the staff base with another female nurse. Each one of them is on the computer as well, looking over notes. First, Christine leaves to prepare the meds for the night.

We sit on the sofa observing the remaining nurse. She's young, hesitant and ill at ease, a fact that doesn't miss my attention. "She's a pushover. Her and Christine will be piss-poor besiegers," I say. She notices both of us and gives us a strained smile before peering down at the computer monitor. We wait and wait. It may be only minutes but it feels like hours. What is going to happen next? I'm hot and stifled by the heat of the ward. I remove my jumper and rub a slight build-up of sweat on my brow.

Martin laughs. "You're not backing out now?" Yet his leg is shaking.

We wait a while longer until the nurse gets up and goes to the door. We both take deep breaths, arms at the side of the sofa ready to move it. We gasp when she walks back to the computer for a momentary glance. Then she goes out of the room, locking the door behind her and walks to the medication room.

We stand up and go over to the door. I try to open it. Am I stupid? It's locked. I rummage for the correct key from Jim's set. I frantically try each key, pressing and forcing them into the keyhole without success. I keep scanning around, hoping that none of the patients will pass us and tell the nurses what we're doing.

Soon, I insert the correct key and unlock the door. I prop it open with a wooden stopper before we go over to the sofa and lift it into the room. After closing the door, I start rummaging through the set of keys again to lock it. But I struggle. I'm taking longer to find the same key and I'm scared somebody will see us.

I clutch tightly at the same key, convinced it'll lock the door.

"Come on, you've already used that key five times and it's not working."

I'm flustered but my muscles tighten in a sense of

MANIC

readiness. "Shut up. I know what I'm doing."

"Relax, breathe," he whispers.

I take a deep breath then gently insert the key I've been trying and lock the door. "There you go," he says.

"Let's get to work," I command.

This is the first time that I have ever been in the staff base. It's tidy and has a scent of alcohol. Martin sits on the computer seat and spins around frantically like a child. The screens of the ward's cameras allow us to view most of the patients lined up in the foyer. We are startled when a door slams loudly. We glance at the screens and notice that Stephanie has left her room and is heading towards us.

I duck, pulling Martin onto the floor. I smile as we both stare at each other. "That's the girl I'm after," I whisper.

Martin sniggers nervously. I put my finger to my lips until it's long enough for her to pass by. Slowly, I raise my head to look at the camera screens. No one is outside the staff base or in the corridors. They're all in the foyer.

Martin looks up at the large monitor on the wall. It has all the room numbers of the ward with three icons with different colours and numbers under them.

"Can you make head or tail of these?" he asks.

I stare at my room and the colours green and yellow and think about what they could mean. I'm aware of Martin's and Colin's rooms and notice they're similar to mine in colour and number. Martin points to a room with two red squares.

"I wonder who's in that room."

It's Stephanie's but I say nothing.

"Anyway, let's find her file," I say.

We rummage through the files on the desk in the hope of finding any personal information we can glean on the other patients, in particular, Stephanie. I grunt low in my throat. We have spent so much effort trying to get into the staff base that we can't fail in the end. Martin tries to reassure me.

"Now, come on, think. If you were a nurse or consultant, where would you keep confidential information?"

"To be honest, Martin, I'd keep it out of view so no passer-by could see it."

"Good, that's why they're not sitting on the desk. So,

MARK BROWNLEE

where would the files be?"

"Cupboards," I cry.

I frantically start opening the doors of the cupboards to see if there are any files but find none. But Martin doesn't think I've searched well enough, so he also checks all the cupboards but finds nothing. There's a pain in my forehead as it throbs and I scream with fists in the air, but Martin quickly quiets me and turns to the camera screens to see if anybody in the foyer has heard me, but they don't seem to.

I go to a corner of the room and throw my hands into the air. I kick a filing cabinet, and with my back against the wall, fall to the floor.

"Niall, you're a genius."

"I'm not due any compliments right now, mate."

"No, look!"

I glance up at the filing cabinet Martin is pointing at. My face lights up and my hand yanks at one of the drawers but it's locked.

"Is there a key in Jim's set that might open them?"

I rummage through the set and eventually find a small key that opens the cabinet. I open a drawer and take out a file. I take out Ramona's file from the top drawer while Martin grabs another. We look at the notes but find it incredibly difficult to read the doctor's handwriting.

I deduce that Ramona has a mental illness from drug abuse, while Martin tells me that Colin has a personality disorder. That I already knew.

"Get this, it says he has a *narcissistic* personality disorder."

"Hey, here's your file," I say. "Let's have a look."

"No," he replies.

"Come on. What have you got to hide?"

"Give me that," he says.

"Come on. Don't you want to know what people have been writing about you? Give it to me."

I grab the file before he gets a chance to read it. Martin glances at one of the camera screens. The nurse is heading down the corridor towards us.

"The nurse is coming. What do we do?" he asks while I

read his file.

"What do we do?" he asks again.

"Don't worry, my friend. I'm sure you can handle that little nurse on your own. Let me know if there are any more of them, then I'll give you a hand."

I read through my file and find out that he has a diagnosis of clinical depression. Cool. Martin is pushing the sofa against the door, ready to keep the nurse out. Her jaw drops when she sees both of us in the staff base. She doesn't know what to do and immediately turns back up the corridor to the medication room. Patients gradually pass us after taking their meds. I continue to go through the files.

"Christopher has schizophrenia. Who knew? I flick through Martin's file and find it's mostly blank of any case notes.

"I guess they don't have much on you. Or maybe they have so much stuff on you they had to start a new file. Where's Stephanie's file?"

He rummages through the filing cabinet but can't find any files with her name on. Suddenly, an alarm goes off. Christine and the other nurses are at the door.

Christine glares right at me. It's disturbing.

"Niall, open this door right now," she yells.

I laugh and give her the fingers.

Soon, a well-built male nurse in his fifties arrives at the scene. Now it's three against two. The nurses open the lock of the door and push us back. We're giving ground. Our feet slip backwards and so does the sofa. The male nurse tries to force his body through the gap in the door. First his hand in, then his arm, then he manages to slide in half of his body.

Martin stands up, causing the door to go inwards, throwing me and the sofa back. Then with lightning speed, I throw a clenched fist at the male nurse's face. Before anybody knows what's happening, the nurse falls back to the corridor floor, clutching his cheek.

Hang on. I just punched somebody in the face. Why did I do that? I guess it was one of those fight-or-flight reactions. I look at Martin who takes a step back from me. Clearly, I've gone too far. My muscles go weak or numb as I turn to the

MARK BROWNLEE

nurses.

Christine and the other nurse move back and attend to the nurse on the floor.

A lull ensues as the alarm stops. I stare at the nurse I punched while Martin shakes his head. What sort of a monster am I? Surely there will be consequences for all this. But I'm here for a reason – to find out why Stephanie is here.

I turn to Martin and nod. "Let's find her file."

But Martin seems to have had enough of reading patients' notes. He stares out at the male nurse who's still disorientated, lying on the floor.

I search in all the cupboards and on the desks until I find Stephanie's file behind the computer monitor. I open it and read. Martin alerts my attention to two male police officers entering the hospital, seen from the camera.

"You need to have a look at this, Niall."

"Hang on, mate. I'm reading."

I'm in the middle of a case note which reads:

"Stephanie said: 'I've never been the same since the day it happened. My whole world was turned upside down and I blame myself for everything. A part inside me died.'"

What happened? Why was her world turned upside down and why does she blame herself? The whole purpose of this was to get answers about why she's here but I've only got more questions.

"Come on, Niall. Help me brace the door," he shouts.

"As I said before, mate, we were always going to lose this war but it was still worth it in the end."

With that, I throw the file into the corner and turn as the police stand outside the door. Christine gives them the key. They unlock the door and push their way into the room. I recoil back into the corner, shaking all over. The two officers easily restrain me with handcuffs. Where was my fight response this time? I guess deep down I'm a real chicken.

The officers stand me up and bring me out of the room, leaving Martin to stand speechless at everything that has happened.

11

THE GIRL

Monday 23rd December

sit shaking all over. I fan the sweat on my face with my hand as it's clammy, and my armpits are wet. I hope those in front of me don't notice. It's like an interview from Hell only there is no hope of getting a job at the end of it, just the avoidance of a criminal charge.

Christine stands beside me before two police officers, one female, and one male who is standing over me with body armour, handcuffs and a pistol. I guess he isn't taking any chances. He moves closer to me and takes out a notepad and pen.

"Now, Mr Alexander. The incident that just took place, which saw a staff member injured, has led to a criminal investigation. The staff member wishes to press criminal

MARK BROWNLEE

charges against yourself. Therefore, can you please state your account of the incident in question?"

I clear my throat. I try to shift the blame to Martin, saying it was his idea. I know I'm lying but I hope I'm convincing. The male officer takes notes and occasionally glances at me while the female officer sits in the corner, with her arms folded and a stern look on her face.

There's silence until the male officer finishes writing. "Whose idea was it to break into the staff base?"

"Martin's. He said he wanted to look at the patients' records."

"Did you want to look at them as well?" the female officer asks.

I shudder then shake my head profusely. A lie that pricks my conscience slightly.

"Can you describe the mental state of Martin during the incident?" the male officer continues.

I turn to the other officer whose gaze is fixed on me. "There is something wrong with Martin, otherwise he wouldn't be in the hospital. We are all here for a reason. I'm sure Martin has his."

"And why are you in the hospital?" the male officer asks.

I sigh. "I've a bipolar disorder."

They turn to each other then the male officer turns back to me. "We have no further questions," they both say.

"Does this mean I'm going to face any charges?"

"We will inform you in due course," the female officer states.

"Surely you must have an inkling whether I'm guilty or not."

"We don't like sharing our inklings," she says as they leave.

I follow them out of the door to the exit while Christine turns left to go back to the staff base. She then returns with a heart monitor.

"What's going to happen to me? Why is that nurse pressing charges against me?"

"I don't know. Police always question whether a suspect has the mental capacity to be responsible for their actions.

MANIC

What I do know is charges made against patients generally don't go very far."

"Could I go to jail or get a criminal record?"

"To be honest, Niall, my guess is nothing will come of it. But you deserve a good scare all the same. I want to do a few checks to assess how well you're doing."

"What sort of checks?"

"Aren't you a curious individual? I want to get your height and weight to find out your BMI."

"Why do you want to find out my BMI? Am I underweight?"

"We are more concerned that you'll be overweight. Now that you've started to take your medication, we want to check for effects. Since you only started complying to medication on Saturday, we won't see any change yet. We're just getting your baseline. A lot of these antipsychotics we put people on often have a side effect of weight gain."

Isn't that great? Now I'll have to try and get Stephanie's attention as Sumoman. I can forget the six-pack and the inguinal crease, although the latter was always ambitious anyway. I'll have more chins than a multi-chinned hippo and more tyres around my chest than a loyalist bonfire.

We enter the medication room and the smell of alcohol immediately hits me. There are charts and posters on the wall while the desktops are uncluttered. There before me are the scales. The digital numbers race up and down before they stop at a hundred and seventy pounds. That means nothing to me so I ask Christine what that is in stones. She runs her finger up and across a chart.

"Twelve stones and one pound."

No, I'm heavier than the last time I weighed myself.

"Now for your height."

I stand where she is gesturing and allow her to measure me. The marker comes down on my head. I step away while Christine takes a note of the result.

"How tall's the weed?"

"Six feet and three inches."

I make a fist pump. "Yes. One inch taller than Edward the Longshanks."

MARK BROWNLEE

"Who?"

"Edward the Longshanks. The English king who got the nickname 'Longshanks' for being so tall."

She shakes her head. "Anyway, I'm working out your BMI and its … 21.2, which is perfectly healthy. We'll monitor it to see if there is any change."

I run to my room. I'll need to start doing as much exercise as I can to offset the weight gain. I do a dozen sit-ups and push-ups. After, I take a shower and then carefully dry myself. Then I take my time deciding what to wear. Still not quite sure what Stephanie wants in a guy but I'm going to find out all the same. I put on my best pair of chinos and Skecher shoes before staring at my naked upper half in the mirror. I wish I had a six-pack but my skinny frame will have to do for now as I pull over my Lou Reed t-shirt of Lou Reed. Hoping that she'll pick up the reference to the song, *Stephanie Says* by The Velvet Underground, because it's been stuck in my head ever since I met her. Of course, I can't be too polished. I need to be a rough diamond – fabulous without trying. I ruffle my hair a little, not too much. I go to leave the room and then I remember I need to put on some aftershave. In this case, Lynx won't do. I've got to pull out all the stops, even though I'm on a budget. Red Diesel's my choice.

I leave and look out for her – she is nowhere to be seen. Maybe she went for a nap; perhaps she was granted leave or is out with visitors. Wherever she is, I'll have to wait.

I go into the canteen where Jim writes an inspirational thought for the day on the whiteboard. Pretentious, if you ask me. Family and friends of patients sit waiting to meet their loved ones and Martin sits at a table on his own reading a book.

"Hey, what have you got there?"

He licks a finger before turning a page. "It's James Edwards' biography."

I smile. "Have you read much of it?"

"Just the first few chapters. The guy is overrated."

"What? You can't be serious."

"I'm dead serious."

"What do you mean?"

MANIC

"It's too early to have a biography written about him before he has even completed his first term in office. We should judge him after. Plus, I'm wary of his time as a preacher; he is one of those evangelical Christians."

"Yeah, but not one of those televangelist guys. He has a lot of potential in uniting the political divide in America."

Martin takes the book off the table and cradles it in his lap. "They always say that at the start, especially when they receive a lot of support. Then they're hated like every lame-duck President when they leave office."

"No, Edwards is different."

Martin raises an eyebrow. "He's just a man."

"The most powerful man in the world. You mark my words. I hope to meet him one day."

Martin rolls his eyes.

"I'm serious. There's something in my bones that tells me I will meet him soon." I know I was wrong about meeting him in the hospital. Still, I honestly believe I will meet him soon and I've got an even greater conviction of this than ever before.

"A gut feeling?" Martin asks.

"Yeah, I guess. Anyway, I was wondering if you knew where Stephanie was?"

"She is doing her daily meditation. You're best not disturbing her until she finishes."

"Don't worry, I won't."

Colin passes by and immediately grins when he sees me. "Hey, how's my favourite future convict? What on earth possessed you to break into the staff base yesterday? Don't worry, I know. A certain female whose name I'll not mention. Did you see her file?"

Martin closes the book and puts it on the table then turns to me. Should I tell him the truth or keep to myself? Well, Stephanie is into me right now so what have I got to lose.

I turn to Colin and nod.

"What did you find out?" he asks.

"Something happened to her. I don't know what but it had a big impact on her."

"Really, I wonder what that was," Colin says.

I smile. "Me too."

MARK BROWNLEE

My eyes widen. Yes, that's it. Edwards. I impress Stephanie by meeting Edwards. Martin might not like Edwards, but Stephanie certainly does, and so do I. Yet how am I to get in touch with the leader of the free world now that I'm in a hospital? I guess I could write to him. Will he even respond, let alone meet me in person? I'm stumped – think. What do I have that Edwards wants? Not much to be honest. What does he want or, more importantly, what does he need? What makes him tick? Could I somehow appeal to his religious sentiments? Could I deceive him by promising him something then informing him of the real purpose of our meeting? How could a small Irish farm with a stream and orchards entice one of the greatest men of our generation? The following in my room is a stab at it.

Dear Edwards, (AKA Théoden, King of Rohan)

On 20th December, the Russians tried to kill you before planning to nuke the world. You are welcome to my home where we can discuss these matters further. It is not overly grand or impressive but I can give you Adam's apple and ale. However, it will depend on which road you take. The narrow back road is found by many using modern technology as their guide; you'll receive the bitter taste of the apple. But if you see and choose the front path by listening to my directions, you'll receive the fresh taste of Adam's ale. When you enter my home, I'll call you master and you can call me your humble servant, for I'm not above you, I'm below you. You might find it difficult to see me for you are the giant, proud elephant while I am the small humble mouse below. If you fear me, decide a place to meet somewhere in the Isle of Ireland for I am a guy of limited wealth and my island is sacred to me.

Yours sincerely,

Niall Alexander (AKA Tom Bombadil)

P.S. There's one other critical matter I would like to talk to you about regarding a girl.

What do I think of my masterpiece? First off, it's not a masterpiece. Most would say it is the rambling of a mad man as is most of my work. But you know what they say – there's a fine line between genius and insanity. I don't think it's crazy or insane. I think it's stupid and immature and that's kind of the

MANIC

only thing that's wrong with me. I do too many stupid and immature things and that's how I ended up in a psychiatric hospital. I know it's a long shot but I'd like to think if I send it to Edwards he *might* (and there needs to be a big emphasis on might) help me out with getting Stephanie. The point is I've conjured up the courage to write something that I hope will lead to a face-to-face encounter with Mr Edwards.

As I finish writing, there's a knock at the door. "Niall, you've got a visitor," Christine says. I pace along the corridor to the staff base where Conor is waiting.

We go to the interview room where we sit. There are plastic holders with mental pamphlets up on the wall to my left. Then behind Conor is a framed photograph with the inspirational quote: 'positive thoughts lead to positive things'. I disagree, unlike the optimist. I like to be optimistic about my pessimism and wonder why he isn't as optimistic.

"How's the farm?" I ask.

Conor reclines back into his chair. "Yeah, the usual. Milking the cows. We started pruning the orchards yesterday. I was mostly putting in silage for cattle today. I suppose you're glad you're in the hospital now and don't have to do any of that sort of stuff."

"True," I lie knowing that I have fleeting hopes of taking over the farm and turning it into a commune for Stephanie.

He stares at me as I tap my knees with my hands. There's something of an awkward silence. I wonder if he is thinking the same thing I am: Mum and Dad. More specifically, is Dad still drinking and is Mum still beaten to a pulp. I make a decision not to talk of that but instead talk about something else.

"I thought I would show you a letter I wrote. You know how big a fan I am of James Edwards."

He smirks. "I wouldn't say you're just a fan; you've become rather obsessed with him."

"Maybe. This is a short letter I want you to send to him for me. If he gets it, I hope he'll decide to meet up with me."

I take out the piece of paper from my pocket and read it to him. "What do you think?"

He nods. "Interesting. I'm not sure it's enough to get him to come to our home, though. More important than that,

MARK BROWNLEE

who's the girl?" he asks with a grin.

"Nobody you know."

He laughs. "Spill the beans."

"Will you post it?" I say through gritted teeth, my body tense.

"Maybe, if you tell me who the girl is."

"She's called Stephanie."

"Come on, a name's not enough. I want details."

I sigh as I release the tension in my body. "She's around the same age as me with long ginger hair. She's doing her A-Levels at the minute. Really into poetry and literature."

"Oh, the airy-fairy type. Very nice."

I roll my eyes before my pulse speeds up again. "Well?"

"Well, what?"

"Will you post the letter?" I ask as heat burns through my body.

"You think I can just post your letter directly to the White House?" he asks as his eyes widen.

"I can't. I'm in the hospital."

"How about you hack into the FBI or something?" he says with a smile.

"You think I should email it?"

He laughs. "Niall, you can post it when you're well. Plus, how do you know Edwards is going to help you get this girl?"

"She likes Edwards."

Okay, I know how the whole idea sounds stupid but it's not impossible. A boy once wrote to the President and commended him on his stance on climate change. The kid was so impressed he said he would donate half of all his weekly pocket money while Edwards was in office. Edwards sent him a letter of reply and it became a minor news story. I know stuff like that rarely happens but they still happen.

"Look, if I get in touch with Edwards, I might impress Stephanie."

"Man, you know nothing about women," he says, shaking his head.

"How did you get Jenny?"

"Not by trying to write to the President of the United States of America. I guess the tried and tested rule is to talk to

MANIC

this girl. It's that simple and be yourself."

Everybody knows talking to her is the key but there's nothing wrong with having a bit of spice, an ace of spades. Edwards will be my ace of spades.

"I'll get Stephanie, you'll see. If you post the letter."

Conor sighs loudly. "Fine, I'll post your letter. Give it to me."

I hand him the letter and he folds it into his coat pocket. "Dad wants me to chat to the nurse to see how you're doing."

He leaves but I anticipate Conor's reaction to the events of last night. Ramona sprints down the corridor, screaming, chased by Jim. I roll my eyes. After fifteen minutes, Conor returns, red faced and glaring.

"You broke into the staff base and looked at confidential patient information. What sort of goat are you? I can't believe I've such a prat of a brother. You've a lot of explaining to do."

I laugh. "It's the girl."

"Niall, this isn't funny," he says with his eyebrows drawing together.

I shrug. "I'll be alright."

"I wish you were alright. Look, will you promise you'll stay out of any further trouble?" he says, leaning towards me.

"Sure," unless reasons mean I have to do otherwise but I don't say this.

"Good. I got to go. The missus will be expecting me home for dinner."

I stand up and nod at him as he leaves. Then I sit down and ponder everything that has happened to me. Most importantly, Stephanie. Where is she? I smile and recline in my chair until Stephanie bursts into the room. "Who do you think you are?" she shouts, pointing a finger at me.

"I don't know what you're talking about," I say, with pain in the back of my throat.

"My file – you read it," she says, glaring at me with flared nostrils.

"I didn't."

"Colin said you did."

"He's lying," I say, my heart now racing.

"Why did you break into the staff base?"

She's got me.

"You haven't got much to say now, have you?" she rants with her arms folded.

I put out both my arms in an apologetic gesture. "I'm sorry."

She sighs, putting her hands down to her sides. "Look, when I first met you, I thought you were a bit strange in a quirky way. But I liked you and thought maybe something could have happened but not now."

"Why?"

Her eyes bulge. "You've no respect for my privacy. I don't want you to know why I'm here and why I'm depressed but you had the nerve to break into the staff base and read my personal notes. How can I respect a guy who doesn't respect me?"

I offer her an embrace. "Stephanie, of course, I respect you."

She recoils, holding up her hands. "No."

I step back from her and silence ensues. She lowers her head and covers her face with her hand before staring at me again.

"I know this will be hard for you to take, but I would appreciate it if you left me alone."

"Stephanie, I ..."

"No, Niall. We're over, for good."

As she leaves, every fibre of my being wants to say something, anything, yet it will only make matters worse. And in light of everything she has told me, the most gut-wrenching, sucker punch thing is knowing there was potential between us, but that it's over. I blew it, not because I humiliated myself with somebody who wasn't interested in me – I've experienced that countless times before – but for the first time in my life, I blew it with somebody who liked me, and it feels like Hell.

12

DAY TRIP

Tuesday 24th December

t's Christmas Eve, and I'm and I'm walking with everybody else to the hospital exit. Jim leads the way with Colin and Stephanie who whispers something into her ear. Whatever it is, it puts her into a fit of laughter. I always thought I would love getting out of this joint, but today all I want to do is lie on my bed and sulk. I mean, it's almost Christmas and I'm stuck in a hospital. I miss my mum, Niamh and Conor. I might even miss Dad. Nah, I would need to be in a pretty bad way for that to happen. The point is I want to be at home right now with most of my family.

Rain drizzles down on us this morning like the pat of a patronising grandparent. Jim told us to bring a coat, which is just as well since the rain is getting heavier. By the time we're outside, everybody has their raincoats and woolly hats on to face the elements. There are ten of us in total with me and Martin at the back, quiet. As we stand in the freezing cold, Jim turns to us.

"We are getting a bus here and it'll drop us off in the car park of the shopping centre and then pick us up after a few hours. Stick together and no wandering off."

"We're not kids," I shout.

"I know, Niall, but you're all here in the hospital for complex reasons. You should be glad you're allowed to get out at all," he retorts.

Colin laughs. "Yeah, Niall."

I sigh. Could this day get any worse? Because it hasn't had the best of starts.

We leave the hospital and get on a grey minibus. Somehow, Martin and I manage to get the back seat whlle Stephanie and Colin sit at the front. The perfect position to torment me. Stephanie laughs at everything Colin says to her. What could he possibly be saying to her that has such an effect? I turn to Martin.

"What do you think of Colin?"

"To be honest, I think very little of him if you ask me."

I nod. "Is he funny?"

Martin tilts his head to the side and frowns. "Why do you say that?"

"Well, he seems to make Stephanie laugh."

"She's probably faking it to be nice."

I wish I could make Stephanie laugh in that way, even if she was faking it. I know I need to be more like a comedian. "What about Spiffy Jenkins?" I ask.

"What about him?"

"He's a funny guy. Girls like funny guys."

"True. But girls our age are searching for good-looking guys, which is why she's after Colin and not you. Look, mate, you blew it; forget about her. I'm sure you'll find somebody else."

Is Martin right? Should I forget her? His suggestion almost convinces me to do so but I can't. I'm not going to give up that easily. Still, my heart feels like it's shrinking and my ribs grow tight, making it hard to breathe.

MANIC

The bus stops in the car park. Colin and Stephanie get out first. It's still raining. He takes off his backpack and out comes a small umbrella which he places over their heads. An umbrella? This guy's seventeen, not some middle-aged English gentleman with a bowler hat and white gloves to go with it. Although there's some pleasure in seeing a gust of wind blow and invert his ridiculous umbrella.

We walk into the shopping centre. The Christmas tree in the centre is covered in far too much multi-coloured tinsel which makes it tacky. The place is busy with last-minute shoppers. I'm in no mood for shopping. The only person I want to buy for doesn't like receiving gifts. This whole day trip is pointless unless I find some other way of appealing to her heart. I know – poetry.

"Martin, do you think I'll impress Stephanie if I write her a poem?"

"Didn't she criticise the poem you wrote in the art room?"

"Yeah, but that was my first time. Now I have a better idea of what she wants. There's that poem from Shakespeare: *Shall I compare you to a summer's day?*"

"I can't say my knowledge stretches beyond that movie *Shakespeare in Love* but isn't that poem you're talking about a dude?"

"Yeah, but there is nothing wrong with being inspired by it. I'll write my poem in iambic pentameter. We need to get to a library and find poems to inspire me to write."

"Why? Can't you just google the poems? I'm sure you can access all the main ones."

"No, we need to go to the library. I can't think here; there is far too much noise and the crowds are making me claustrophobic. Come on, Martin."

"Alright, alright. We'll leave the group when Jim is distracted."

We both watch Jim like watchmen waiting on the dawn. We enter a shop and when everybody else comes in, we hold back by the doors and then exit without anybody noticing. We run through the shopping centre but find it's so congested in places that we have to elbow our way through the crowds until we get out. We rush out onto the footpath and before we cross the road, a taxi drives past us through a puddle, drenching us. Yes, my day is indeed getting worse.

We run to the library and march through the sturdy bookshelves. It's quiet with very few people in it. I go to the poetry section and scan the poets like Burns, Donne, Yeats, Heaney and Wordsworth. I keep reading through their works, but nothing seems to speak or inspire me.

"Come on, Niall. I'm bored."

Martin may be frustrated but so am I by our pointless journey. I slam a book closed and throw it on the floor, which turns the heads of other members of the public and receives a frown from the librarian, who lowers her glasses down her nose. Then I look at a leaflet on a table and my eyes light up. The Ulster Museum is exhibiting Alexandros of Antioch's Venus de Milo statue and today is the last day.

"Martin, we need to go to this."

"So, we go to the library, now the museum. What's next? The theatre?"

"No, I need to go. If I sit in the museum and see this statue, it will inspire me to write a poem for Stephanie."

"Alright,"

We make our way to the Ulster Museum. We walk along Botanic Avenue and pass *The Empire*. They have stand-up comedy this evening. If only I had a better sense of humour – girls love funny guys.

"Martin, are you sure you don't know any jokes you could share with me?"

"You still want to make Stephanie laugh?"

I nod.

"Well, it's not just about knowing funny jokes; it's about having comic timing and good delivery."

True. But is there something for being so bad it's good. "What about the lovable rogue? Like Winston Churchill. He went far doing that."

"Careful, you did say Stephanie was a socialist. Plus, the lovable rogue is like marmite. You either love him or you hate him. What did you have in mind?"

"Well, it's Christmas. How about I dress up as Santa Clause, shouting, 'Ho, ho, ho, Merry Christmas'. Then I share a

MANIC

Christmas joke, and then my ace of spades is my poem."

"It could work. But make sure when you're pretending to be Santa you say 'ho' and not 'hoe', if you catch my drift. You want to state you're just happy and not presuming her occupation. There was a Santa in America who got the sack because women commented his 'ho, ho, ho' was more 'hoe, hoe, hoe', if you know what I mean. Plus, if you're going for Christmas humour, I'm assuming you mean cracker jokes, which we could find on the internet. Who knows, Stephanie might like them. But I think you're right. If you write a good poem, it could be your ace of spades. But first things first, we need to get you a Santa suit."

We stroll around Botanic Avenue, searching for somewhere that sells Santa suits. Sure, it's Christmas after all. We find an old charity shop which happens to have a Santa suit on the mannequin in the window. As we enter, there is a musty old smell. Most of the people inside are female and of a particular vintage. I ask the shopkeeper how much the Santa suit is. She says it's a fiver – bargain. I ask if I could try it on. She paces to the shop window in no rush, removes the suit from the mannequin and hands it to me. I grab it and rush to the nearest changing cubicle, chuck the suit on the ground and turn to pull the curtain. I stick my thumb up and give a goofy smile to Martin who laughs.

I stand in front of the mirror as I undress. Not quite Mr Universe, more like cringe central to be perfectly honest. But for once I'm confident I can pull this whole thing off or at least be able to take it if it didn't go my way. The suit is baggy when I put it on. What am I going for here? A fat Santa or a sexy Santa? I'd have better luck as a sexy one so I'll ditch the beard and no pillows to bulk me out.

I open the curtain and throw my hands out in a jazz hands gesture to Martin. "Ta-da."

He's silent with his arms folded at an angle. What does he think of me? More importantly, what will Stephanie think of me?

He frowns. "She might like this."

I nod. I can take those odds. "Do you have a bag for these?"

MARK BROWNLEE

"Sure, you can put it in my backpack."

I change back into my normal clothes and put the Santa suit into Martin's backpack. When we leave, I say goodbye to the shopkeeper and run towards the museum.

We head along Botanic Avenue, past the Presbyterian theological college and into Queen's University. I've always wanted to go to university and have the government give me a loan to get an education and live a life free from my parents. We stop outside the university library, out of breath after sprinting. We're now outside the gate of Botanic Gardens. We walk through it as we get our breath back.

It's winter so there are no plants outside but there's some life in the palm house conservatory. It's no longer raining but the wind is chilly. I rub my hands together and blow on them. Martin flails his arms up in the air and whacks his hands against his shoulders, which leaves passers-by stopping and staring. He smiles at me.

"A little trick my dad taught me to keep warm. Yep, you do look ridiculous, but boy does it work."

"Hey, let's go into the palm house conservatory and check out all the plants and flowers."

"Sorry, not really into all that flowers and nature stuff."

"Suit yourself," I say as I go into the conservatory and feel much-needed heat in my fingers. I walk around looking at all the trees, flowers and plants on display. A bunch of orange roses remind me of Stephanie's hair. Girls appreciate flowers and nature. I must get her some flowers but I don't have time today. If only Stephanie was here now or we were both at The Argory near Armagh. That would be awesome.

When I feel warmth again in my fingertips, we rush to the museum and enter. People are congregating in the cafe area to our left and in the gift shop to our right. We go into the main building and think about where the statue of Venus is. I run over to the desk and ask. A middle-aged woman looks up from her computer and takes off her glasses. She tells me which floor and gives me directions but says I need to be quick as the museum is closing soon. Before I rush off, Martin gestures to me.

"Look, you go on ahead and write your poem. I'm going to

MANIC

wait in the cafe."

"Okay."

I run up the stairs to the correct floor for the history section. I peer around the exhibits until I come to the statue of Venus. There is a chair conveniently situated below the statue. I stare at it for a few moments; I'm in total awe of its magnificence. I write my poem based on what I see. Yet I take liberties. The Venus in this statue has her hair tied back. The Venus I want would have hair dangling down to her shoulders. Starting from the head, I make my way down the body. As I finish, there is an announcement that the museum will close in ten minutes. I read over what I've written and well, I have to say, I've impressed myself. If this doesn't persuade Stephanie to be my girl, nothing will.

I sprint to the cafe where Martin sips on a glass of coke. I walk up to his table.

"We need to meet up with the rest of them before the bus leaves."

"Let me finish my drink."

He downs it and we both leave the museum to a complete downpour. We reach Jim, who is by no means impressed that we ditched the rest of them. Stephanie is still laughing at everything Colin is saying, which infuriates me. I start to doubt whether my poem will convince Stephanie to take me back. We make our way back to the hospital where I spend several hours editing and rewriting the poem.

After dinner, I get myself ready to make my move. I stand in front of the mirror, dressed in my Santa suit and wonder whether I need the white beard again. I don't. What will Stephanie think of all this? There is only one way to find out. I leave and walk along the corridor until I'm standing outside her room. I take a deep breath and knock twice. For some reason, probably the adrenalin, I'm filled with a real sense of confidence. This is going to work. After a while, someone inside comes to the door. It opens to Stephanie, frowning.

"Ho, ho, ho! Merry Christmas. I have something I want to say, so hear me out."

"I don't want to hear it, Niall."

MARK BROWNLEE

I flinch slightly then shake my head. "What did Adam say before Christmas?"

"Niall, I don't know and don't care."

"It's Christmas, Eve."

Okay, so she didn't like me being Santa or the Christmas joke. But even Martin agreed my poem was my ace of spades. So here goes.

"*The Statue of Venus*
Your frame stands and rays its beauty now
like a monument standing proud and tall,
with hair descending precipice of head
like flaming waterfalls that around you flow.
Your face is smooth and warm to touch and stroke.
Its tender colour now before my eyes.
Your neck is like a tower adorned with jewels,
your shoulders are protruding out below
they are an arch that dangle arms of pink
with delicate and dainty hands that hang.
Your crimson lips are soft as silk to taste.
I kiss your cheek that tastes and looks of peach."

I smile as I gaze into Stephanie's big blue eyes even though they're narrow. Her arms are folded. She turns around and goes back into her room where Colin is standing there with his arms folded. I close my eyes. This can't be happening.

13

CHRISTMAS DAY

Wednesday 25th December

ello, Niall. How are you doing today," Christine asks in the interview room, which is one of the rooms staff felt they couldn't be bothered to decorate for Christmas. Grinches, the lot of 'em. It's not that I'm really into Christmas but more decorations might have done something in getting rid of the blues I'm currently experiencing.

I sigh. "To be honest, I'm not great given the circumstances."

"I understand. Nobody wants to be in the hospital on Christmas Day, not even me."

I nod.

"I just wanted to touch base and see if you are doing okay."

MARK BROWNLEE

"I don't need to be here anymore," I say. I mean, I haven't had an episode ever since I started taking the medication. Okay so it's only been four days since taking medication, still I'm desperate to get out of this place.

She smiles. "Give it a few more weeks and if you improve and remain stable, there's no reason why we'll need to keep you here."

"Does that mean I'll be off school?"

"Yes, but hopefully you won't miss too many days."

I'm glad I became unwell over the Christmas holidays. Fewer questions will be asked over my long absence from school with less lying on my part. I mean, I could casually say to my mates I was off because I had the blues and shrug at whatever they say to that. Them thinking I was depressed would be better than them knowing the truth – that I've been totally off my rocker with symptoms of psychosis.

There's a knock at the window. We both turn. It's Mum. "It seems you've a visitor. I'll leave the two of you to it."

We take a trip around Ormeau Park and sit on a summer seat. We're both silent as is Belfast so it seems. There's a lone robin chirping and moving from tree to tree and some leaves still decaying on the ground. Mum closes her eyes and takes a deep breath. There's a bruise around her ear although the previous one on her face has faded, probably because of all the makeup she has on. I grit my teeth and my body tenses. I know exactly how she got it but I'm also aware of her routine denial of the cause. I want to talk to her without inviting her to immediately come to Dad's defence but even attempting to talk about the subject, no matter how softly you tread, demands that you have to bite the bullet.

"Mum, what's happening between you and Dad?

She says nothing.

I sigh and shake my head. "Have you looked at yourself this morning? What's this?" I say, pointing to her ear.

She laughs hesitantly. "Oh, it's nothing. I knocked myself into the edge of a door. My own stupid fault."

"Don't talk trite," I say, which makes her face turn white and then I realise I'm getting angry with the victim rather than the perpetrator of the crime. I take a deep breath and let the

MANIC

fire in my belly abate.

"Your father's been under a lot of stress recently with the farm. Milk prices have dropped and all the expenses keep going up."

"But other farmers are experiencing the same pressure. That doesn't mean they lash out on their wives." Why does she always have to make excuses for him?

She looks down at her hands and fidgets with her fingers. "You know farming doesn't come naturally to him."

"So, what. That doesn't mean he can take it out on people he should hold dear," I say in a deepening tone as my pulse speeds up and my muscles quiver.

"Has he been drinking much?" I add. Do I need to even ask?

Mum pauses.

"Has he?"

Her silence speaks volumes. I clench both my fists and hold them down hard on my quads.

"Mum, this has got to stop. You need to tell somebody."

The mere suggestion makes Mum's nostrils flare and her eyes bulge. "I will do no such thing, and I forbid you, Niamh or Conor from saying anything too."

I throw my hands up in the air to appease her anger until she calms down.

It's not like it's a closely guarded secret. Everybody with half a brain would notice her bruises and put two and two together. I'm surprised nothing has been done about it yet. I know if I say this I will only be adding fuel to the fire. She says nothing, merely looking at the ground.

"You wouldn't understand, Niall. You've never been in love before."

I'm silent. I can't understand how love can make my mum the way she is.

There is another awkward silence.

"You know this is where your father and I had one of our first dates."

I roll my eyes. "Mum, I don't want to hear this."

She sighs and closes her eyes. "I remember it like yesterday."

I'm sure Dad was a very different man from the man he is now.

She opens her eyes again. "You know … I still love him and don't you ever forget that. I will always love him," she says.

It doesn't faze me. "Even if it hurts you?" I ask.

"With love, you always experience an element of hurt. It's the price you have to pay. It's probably something you don't understand yet. In time, you will."

I understand better than she thinks. Still, I could never understand why she would allow herself to be beaten to a pulp for love. Has she no self-respect? She's in a harmful relationship. No, it's become more than that. It's dangerous and yet she seems to remain so carefree and oblivious to it all. She is the one that bears the brunt. Conor, Niamh and I have mostly been spared but that could always change. We are the witnesses of trauma but saying that eludes who the real victim is in this whole situation: Mum. I would understand if one day she left the four of us to start a life somewhere else. Can't she see it's love that makes me want her to do that? Will she ever leave him? After hearing her today, I don't think she ever will.

We make our way back to the hospital. There is more commotion as Ramona paces about the ward.

"I'm Ramona, Mary Reynolds," she raves. She stares at different staff members then she greets me while Mum goes to see Doctor Henson and the other nurses.

"I'm Ramona, Mary Reynolds," she says. With a frown on her face, she offers her hand to me.

I'm really not in the mood for this but she persists. "What's your name?"

"I'm Niall Alexander," I shout angrily.

She recoils slightly then turns away and starts to march back to the staff base while singing the Taylor Swift song, *Look What You Made Me Do.*

Why the am I here? I really can't go on.

Colin walks up to me, smiling. "So how was your Christmas Day?"

Why does he have to remind us all that we're stuck in a hospital on the one day of the year we would all like to be home the most. As I'm thinking this, I look at the half-

MANIC

decorated tree in the corner of the canteen. Yes, that's right, a half-decorated Christmas tree. Clearly, the person responsible just thought after a while, *You know, I really want the patients to feel valued and get into the Christmas spirit.* Then thought, *nah*, and decided to leave it half-finished. And to top it off, the lights on it don't work. So how was Christmas, Colin? It was terrible, just like yours and everybody elses, including staff, who are stuck in this place. But of course, I don't say this and because I say nothing, Colin continues to speak.

"You were out. Who did you spend your Christmas Day with?"

"My mum."

"Oh, so you're a mummy's boy, are you?"

"Shut up."

He laughs. "I'll spend it with Stephanie she gets back. Aw." He points at Christopher and Ramona hugging each other, Ramona's chin resting on Christopher's head.

"How romantic. I'd call that a good omen for Stephanie and me. Don't you think, Niall?" he smiles and walks off.

I move past Christopher and along the hallway to Mum. She makes her way towards me.

She smiles. "The staff say you haven't had any episodes since taking your medication. Surely that's a step in the right direction?"

I nod and press my lips tightly together to keep me from smiling. It is good news and hopefully, it means they'll discharge me soon. But let's not forget it's Christmas Day and I'm stuck in a hospital. I take deep calming breaths. I fail to experience any happy thoughts of one day leaving the hospital, just the realisation of being stuck in this place.

We embrace each other. I wrap my long arms around her like a sloth, and she kisses me on the cheek before we separate.

"Goodbye, Niall," she says with a beaming smile.

I nod again only this time I can't hide my smile. She pinches my cheek.

"It's nice to know the spirit of Christmas still exists in places like this," she says before I watch her leave.

I head to my room to find solace. As I do so, I once again

MARK BROWNLEE

am intrigued by the information monitor in the staff base. I peer in through the glass panel of the door and try to figure out the four coloured squares under each room icon. The colour red suggests the occupant has a more severe condition or requires more attention or support. I stare at the monitor, at Stephanie's icons – they're all red. The door opens and out comes Christine.

"Is everything alright?"

I nod and turn around, making my way to the lobby area where Colin and Martin are playing table tennis. I take a seat that faces them and watch the game that Martin eventually wins. My head moves to the left and to the right with each rally. Since Martin is the winner, he plays me. As Colin leaves, I stand up and lift the bat.

"Where is Stephanie?" I ask.

"She's still not back."

I sigh as my anger abates and there is a slither of hope that I might still win Stephanie. You probably know how I plan to do it. I turn to Martin.

"Do you think I could beat her in table tennis?" Yes, desperate times call for desperate measures but I still want that kiss and I need to be on top of my game to ever have a hope of beating her.

"Maybe," Martin replies.

Maybe I should consider something else entirely. I scratch my head. "What about chess? I'm good at chess."

"She prefers table tennis, mate."

I wonder if I will be able to persuade her to play a game of chess today when she comes back? I smile as she walks past Martin. There's only one way to find out. Martin turns around to her and then nods at me. I rush out into the corridor.

"Hey, Stephanie."

She stops and turns around to me.

I smile. "How was your Christmas?" Yeah, I know a stupid question but it was the only thing I could think of at the time.

"Fine," she says emotionlessly. "How was yours?"

"I was wondering if you would like to play a game of chess with me?"

She sighs. "Sorry, I'm shattered this evening."

MANIC

"How about tomorrow?" I say. Colin stands behind her, his arms folded.

"I'm getting discharged tomorrow."

I feel a sudden heaviness that expands in my core as my chest tightens. "Why didn't you tell me earlier?"

There is a reddening of her face and her lips curl. "You aren't exactly my boyfriend, are you?"

Colin laughs. I know I'm not but surely there was and still is something between us. Surely she can't think there's nothing.

I tremble. "Can we still be friends?" I ask with a feeling of coldness and a churning stomach.

"Actually, Niall. I would prefer it if we weren't," she says, turning and walking away from me.

What? No. This can't be happening. I try to follow her but Colin stands in my way, allowing her to leave.

14

DESPAIR

Thursday 26th December

he next day, we stand in the foyer to say farewell to Stephanie. She's got a large purple suitcase. She hugs Colin for a long time, her eyes closed. It's so long, their embrace turns them on the spot. Colin's eyes open and he smiles at me until they break apart. There's a burning sensation in my chest as I clench my teeth. My stomach hardens and my breaths become faster and coarser. I want to lash out and hit him but I know that wouldn't be good for anybody. I try to act normal as he stares at me. I release the tension in my jaw, take a deep breath and count to ten inside myself.

Then Stephanie turns to me and my insides melt. I swallow to relieve the dryness of my mouth. I'm lightheaded and even have goosebumps sliding along the back of my neck.

MANIC

"Goodbye, Stephanie," I stutter.

"Goodbye, Niall," she says with hesitation in her voice.

She walks along the corridor to the exit. Is this the last time I'm ever going to see the most beautiful girl I have ever known? The nurse lets her out, and I stare until she is entirely out of view. Then Christine comes to my side.

"I would like to have a word with you."

I walk to the interview room where I sit in front of her. Will they discharge me soon? Will I be able to see Stephanie again? I bite the bullet.

"When Doctor Henson comes back, can you let him know I'm ready to leave the hospital?"

"You're not ready to leave yet."

I know I'm not, but I'm desperate to get out of this place right now.

"Please?" I say with a pain in my chest.

"You're not fit enough to leave the hospital yet."

"Please, I can't stay here?" I cry with a sore throat from all my pleading and begging.

"Niall, you're getting better but you must stay in hospital to guarantee a full recovery."

"A full recovery?" The words stir something in my belly. "You think recovery is more conducive in this place?" I say through gritted teeth and as heat burns through my body,

"You haven't been well, and I understand you're hurt because Stephanie was discharged today."

Oh, Great. Even she knows.

"I've read your notes, and I don't want a repeat of what happened two years ago."

I can't believe she knows about that too. I wonder how much she knows about that? Then the flashbacks flood my brain. Dad's fists, the bruises they left and the tree. The garden sycamore with its broad high branches. I clench my fists and then release them as if I'm holding the rope I thought was going to end it all. I have to say I misjudged Christine. I didn't know she knew all that.

"We are aware of your bipolar disorder but if your mood doesn't change, we'll give you a small dose of antidepressants to get you through this difficult time."

I feel tears run down my cheeks. "Please, let me go home. I want to go home."

"I'm sorry. We are trying to do what's best for you."

My heart is pounding and I grind my teeth. "There is no point continuing this conversation."

I storm out of the room and slam the door behind me. I try to regain my composure. I'm no doubt a mess to Jim who is passing by.

"Are you alright?" he asks, a concerned look on his face.

"Fine," I lie.

"I have something to show you."

We walk into the foyer. Jim leads me to the board that has the values Stephanie and I had come up with for the hospital.

"You and Stephanie certainly have a way with words. I'm sure you'll keep in touch with her."

I ignore what he says and continue to stare at the ideas we came up with that day. I remember how I felt. The day I first got to know Stephanie and more about myself, even if I was angry with her. A day where I wasn't caught up with my past, and I could be at peace with who I was. I glance over the values. They're all characteristics I long for in myself. The definition of faith catches my eye. 'Faith is something that brings meaning to your life, and provides us with peace, hope, courage and true fulfilment.' These were mainly Stephanie's words, written at a time when I had courage and peace, but at present, my body is shaking in despair. I read the words for courage, 'There is no courage without fear. The fearless have no courage for they have no fear. Courage is when we rise above fear.' These were my words. Then the lyrics of the song *Home* by Edward Sharpe & Magnetic Zeros comes onto the radio. The chorus is stuck in my head and plays over and over again. It's about being home with the person you love.

"Maybe you should do some occupational therapy. We're about to do some gardening."

Gardening in winter? But I turn to Jim and nod. We walk to the door that leads to the garden outside. Jim goes and asks other patients if they're interested while I stand alone. Soon, Colin, Martin and a few others are standing out as well. Nobody

MANIC

says anything. Colin catches my glance and smirks. Once Jim has everybody, we go outside.

It's a cold winter's day with overcast skies. Over the past two weeks, there has been a lot of rain and the ground is soaking. The garden consists of a large patio area with numerous ceramic flowerpots. There is a small grass area where a few trees grow. There're weeds stuck in the gaps between the bricks of the patio, which we remove.

I find an orange rose faded and practically dead in a flowerpot. It reminds me of Stephanie's hair. I bend down to sniff its shrivelled head and inhale a weak scent that fills me with delight. For a brief moment, I forget all my problems. I try to pick it up. I clutch the stem and a thorn pierces my palm. I yelp. Life might be a bed of roses, yet roses have thorns. I chuck it on the ground and stamp on it.

Then I do some weeding. I find it a tough task, continually going about on our hands and knees, removing weeds that will probably grow back again come springtime. But I can't deny that the exercise makes me feel better, even if it is only a little. Once finished, Jim tells us the purpose of the exercise is to show we all have recurring problems and weaknesses in our lives, but the important thing is to be determined to stay on top of them. I wonder whether I'll be able to stay on top of mine?

"Okay, everybody. Let's go to the art room and do some work there," Jim says.

Once everybody gets a seat, Martin assembles a metal motorbike.

"Now, Colin. I think he could do some artwork. I really enjoyed your last piece," Jim says.

Colin shrugs. Clearly, artwork wouldn't give him any street cred with his mates outside but here he knows it's good therapy. Oh, you're probably thinking I've gone soft on Colin. I haven't. I still think he's an idiot but I'm really surprised at how he has bought into occupational therapy.

So Colin does some artwork. And me? Well, I probably look as blank as the page before me.

"How about you write some poetry?" Jim asks.

Right now, I need to express myself with a filter. To create some uplifting stuff about how great life is.

"I don't feel like it."

I'm scared of what's on my mind. The thought of ending it all is too prevalent. Jim smiles as I struggle.

"What about Stephanie? Write a poem or something about her."

I stare down at the blank page. There was that poem about Stephanie and the relationship I had with her. I don't blame her. Maybe she has legitimate reasons for why she doesn't want to be my friend? But why? I just want to be her friend – nothing more. Well, at least for now. Is she struggling with her illness in the same way I'm struggling with mine? Well, she was in the psychiatric hospital, and you read in her file that she had had a traumatic experience one day in the past. Will she take or attempt to take her own life? No, she's of stronger stuff. Still, maybe she's hurting or struggling like me. I'm going to write something about her. I rewrite, from memory, my poem entitled the Statue of Venus. It isn't long before I hand it to Jim. I stare at him as he reads it. I smile when his eyes light up.

"This is fantastic," he says.

I turn to Colin and ask what he's working on and he hands me his work. I glare at it for some time while he sits with arms folded, pleased with himself. To me, he has every reason to be – it's a well-produced piece of work yet at the same time, it's simple. He has used white chalk to create a light so bold and encompassing, it has strong religious connections to it. What I find off-putting is what is written underneath – 'the dark light'. Some would say it's an oxymoron; to me, it's a contradiction. How can light be dark? Colin must have bought into the empty platitudes of hope and optimism we are always spoon-fed in occupational therapy. I don't want to be optimistic. I want to be realistic.

I hold up the work to Colin and smile. "I thought I saw the light, but it was an oncoming train."

Colin says nothing. "Come on, Colin worked hard on that," Jim says.

"I have no doubt. It's beautiful. I question the over-optimistic message. Are you spiritual, Colin?" I ask.

MANIC

He frowns. "I dunno. Sort of."

"Close enough. You've an eastern religion vibe going with this piece, which I love. The words 'the dark light'? That's a load of trite."

Jim gasps. "Niall, I can't believe what I'm hearing. How can you be so insensitive? The art room is a safe place for people to express themselves."

"I'm doing just that," I say.

"You're not allowing Colin to. You've offended him."

"Have I offended you?" I ask.

He smiles and shakes his head. Jim is still not happy and demands that I apologise to him.

"Apologise for what? I was only speaking my mind. Why are you so sensitive and uptight about things? You need to chill."

"Niall, apologise now," Jim says, lowering his head with his hands on his hips, holding a hunched posture.

"No," I say, tilting my head back and folding my arms. My chest throbs and my ribs tighten as my thoughts are now clouded by frustration and anger.

"Niall, if you don't apologise, I am going to ask you to leave," he says, dropping his shoulders.

I huff then leave.

Why did Jim get so uptight with what I said? I was only speaking the truth. I need to find some way of relaxing. Stephanie valued the relaxation sessions. She was Jim's star pupil and often found it easy to meditate without any instruction. If only I could relax and clear my mind, I would be more able to think straight.

I go through the foyer and along the corridor to the family room where there are papers and magazines strewn on the floor. I set them on a desk and sit in the middle of the room. I spend fifteen minutes in meditation. There is a loud knock at the door. Before I can respond, the door opens and in comes Colin.

"Hey, mate. Hope I'm disturbing you. I just came to say Stephanie thinks you're pathetic."

Thanks for the compliment, Colin.

"I've got more to offer her than a weasel like you."

114

He moves in closer. It reminds me of the rare times Dad would give me a hiding instead of Mum, when he was drunk. The flashbacks rush back into my head as Colin punches me in the face. I recoil in pain and bend over, clenching my face. I turn towards him and receive another fist to the face that leaves me on the floor. Still conscious, yet phased by the blow that disorients me, I struggle to stand up and before I can get my bearings, I receive a blow to the face and then to the stomach which forces me to the floor. I lie for several moments. When I open my eyes and look around the room, Colin is gone. The pain on the left side of my face is unbearable. It's numb as if I've been electrocuted. Should I retaliate? Come on, Colin is a six-foot-six beast. I don't stand a chance. I feel a pulse in my throat as I take wheezing breaths thanks to Colin winding me. My head is spinning and I struggle to lift my heavy limbs and walk along the corridor to my room.

"Niall, are you alright?" Christine asks. "You look terrible. How did you get that bruise on your face?"

"I banged my head against the wall. My own stupid fault." Great. Now I sound like my mum. I guess that means Colin is Dad.

So, what does hiding from Colin tell you? It tells you, you are a weakling, a pathetic skid mark of a guy that can't even stand up for himself. Is it any wonder Stephanie isn't interested in me? I'm nobody. An idiot, and there is nothing I can do to change that. Some say they feel numb when they're down in the dumps. My feelings aren't numb; on the contrary, they're heightened. I feel twice as heavy and find it difficult to move. My head pounds inside me as I clench my temples. I'm such an idiot. My heart aches so much that it squeezes my chest. There's a thickening in my throat.

I sit at the canteen table, losing track of time, with Martin and Colin. All is quiet; none of the patients speak. I frown at the noisy rattle of metal forks and knives. The verbal silence is torture, the noise of cutlery is irritating, and I want to retch at the stench of alcohol. I'm alone, stuck, and can't get out of this prison of a body.

I recycle the same thoughts over and over again: she's gone; I'm a prat, I'm a prat, I'm such an idiot. Everything is your

MANIC

fault, Niall. You are the only one to blame. Things seem to be happening too fast for me to process them. My emotions aren't numb. No, the emotions make me numb to everything else. The mental anguish is my only emotion; everything else disappears. Only distorted observations of things around me hang me by a thread to this world. A world I no longer want to be a part of. I know if I cut that thread, I'll be free; I'll be at peace. There will be a release to all my pain.

I want to talk to somebody but nobody in the hospital will understand. The only person who would understand is gone. I'm such an idiot. Am I too messed up? Too far gone? It's simple – I'm just not good enough? As I mentally shut down, there is a growing conviction inside me that there is only one thing to do to this mess. End it.

It was two years ago. I could still feel the rope running through my hand as I steadied the stool and tightened the noose around my neck after clumsily tying the rope onto the horizontal beam that ran across the garage roof. I kicked the stool and fell into position. The rope stung my neck like a bunch of nettles. My legs dangled in mid-air as I struggled. My lungs and mouth gasped, wondering which breath would be my last. Then the rope started to loosen and suddenly I fell to the floor. My failure further fuelled my despair and desire to die.

Then it dawned on me one day to google how to tie a noose. I tried a second time. I was able to tie a knot and put it around my neck and I tied the end to a tree. I fell into a position where my feet were slightly off the ground. My backside was against the trunk, and I started to strangle. Seconds passed as I choked and my body spasmed. My eyes closed but my mum came and undid the noose. I wish things had been different.

I scoop some food up with my fork and throw it down onto my plate. I repeat this several times before letting out a sigh. Everybody is so quiet and at ease. Colin is shovelling mashed potato into his mouth like a starving wolf and Martin has an appetite as well. Not me.

I want to vomit looking at the food on my plate. I pause for a moment and stare at a knife. Can this end my life? It's blunt, yet if I'm determined enough, I can probably slit my wrist

MARK BROWNLEE

with it. I take a drink of water.

I grab the blade, hold it up my sleeve and walk along the corridor to my room.

I enter my en suite bathroom and lock the door behind me. I place my back against the door and allow myself to slide down against it until I sit on the floor, head bowed. Can I do this? I take a deep breath and pull the knife out from my sleeve. I stare at it, place the cutting edge across my wrist and pull it across. I hold in a scream as a mark is left, but there is no blood. I try again only this time I press the blade further into my wrist before making the slice. I slice again, deeper and faster. I cry. I grit my teeth as the next slice is more vicious than the two before. I have three fresh marks across my wrist. Surely another will cut open a vein or artery. The knife is placed on my wrist now and I'm more determined than ever to end everything. With one deep slice, I try to cut open a vein. The pain of it makes me let out a scream. Seconds later, there's a voice from outside, "Niall? Niall, are you alright?" I try to stand up but fall to the floor, and my vision goes blurry.

15

RECOVERY

Friday 27th December

open my eyes and find I'm in a hospital bed. I clutch my left arm which is now bandaged up and let out a yelp. To my right, Stephanie is sitting reading a book which she immediately closes and comes to my bedside when she sees I'm awake.

"Colin told me the news. Niall, what were you thinking? Trying to take your own life."

Slightly dazed, I turn to her. "I took it badly when you said you didn't want to be my friend." To be honest, it was more to the fact that Colin beating me up reminded me of all the trauma I had experienced seeing my dad beat my mum and occasionally me. Those were the triggers for my sense of helplessness and suicide attempts in the past and again now. But I can't tell her that – it will only make me look weak.

MARK BROWNLEE

She frowns. "I never thought you would react this way."

The door opens and Christine appears. "So, you're finally awake. I'll let Doctor Henson know," she says, turning around then leaving the room.

Stephanie looks at me with a smile which turns to a frown. "Niall, would you be happy with us being friends?"

"Of course, I'd be happy with us being friends …"

She raises a hand. "No. Hear me out. Friendship with me isn't a stepping stone to a relationship but a friendship and nothing more. If you want to be my friend, you're going to have to realise that."

"I see."

"So, can we be friends? Nothing more?"

I try my best to put on a smile. "Yeah, nothing more." Really, for me, friendship with Stephanie will always be a stepping stone to a relationship. But she doesn't need to know that. Just being friends with her isn't exactly what I want but what other choice do I have? It's that or nothing.

"Can I get your number, friend?" I ask.

"No," she replies. "You can add me on Facebook. Stephanie O'Reilly is my profile name."

There's a slight creak as the door opens again and Doctor Henson, with a large folder, comes in.

"I would like to have a word with Niall, alone please." His words are directed to Stephanie.

She nods. "Sure."

She leaves while Doctor Henson sits at my bedside and crosses his legs. He puts on his glasses before opening a file and spends a few minutes reading, making the odd noise like "mmmm" or "yes" occasionally. He frowns and shakes his head. Once finished, he places the file on the floor and turns to me.

"You certainly had an eventful day yesterday."

I'm not sure if he is making a statement or asking a question.

"Thankfully, the nurses got to you in time. How are you?"

"Not great." I mean, what does he expect me to say? That I'm ecstatic? Over the moon? Couldn't be better? I feel terrible and numb as if a boxer has carefully punched every single part of my body. My head is dizzy and there's still a sharp pain

MANIC

where the knife went across my wrists.

"We hope you'll recover. We've increased your antidepressants, only slightly as there is a chance you'll become psychotic if we increase them too much. You'll feel a difference after a week or so. We'll continue to monitor any changes in your mood in case we have to adjust your medication. Now you need to rest." He stands up then leaves the room.

I lie back on the bed and close my eyes. When I open them, Stephanie is sitting in the armchair reading T.S. Eliot's *Four Quartets* and pretends not to notice me, so I cough. She smiles and then, licking a finger, turns a page, unable to hide a smile.

"You're reading some poetry. I remember you recommended Billy Collins. Would you suggest any other famous poets?"

"That poem you wrote about me as the Statue of Venus wasn't half bad, although I wasn't sure about you comparing me to a statue. If you want to write poems in a strict meter, I'd recommend poets like William Cowper and John Donne."

"You must be really into your poetry."

"I am. I want to be a lecturer in English literature one day."

"It would be great to meet up sometime when we're both out of the hospital."

Stephanie smiles. "Maybe, friend."

"So, it's a *platonic* date?"

"You're cute. We'll have to see. You'll have to write me a sonnet or a poem that's got a strong meter in it. Now you can be quite a player. Can't you see I'm reading Eliot here?" she laughs.

"There's one thing I'd like to tell you, Stephanie."

"What is it?"

My mouth suddenly goes dry and my hands become clammy. What I'm about to say won't be well received.

"You can't go out with Colin."

"Why?" she retorts angrily.

Why? Because he's a bully like my dad and if Colin is Dad that means Stephanie is Mum. I want to spare her the misery my mum has to go through every day. But I know Stephanie will see it as too intrusive so I show discomfort to her glare by looking away.

"This is why I was always doubtful of us ever being friends."

"Of course, we can be friends."

"Only if Colin is not my boyfriend?"

"Well ..."

"Niall, I came because I thought part of the reason why you tried to kill yourself was that we couldn't be friends."

"It was a factor. But it wasn't the main reason."

"I'm going to do something you never did to me. I'm going to respect your personal boundaries by not asking why you tried to take your life."

"Stephanie, I'll always want to be your friend even if you end up marrying Colin. But he's not right for you." Although to be fair, if she did marry Colin I'm sure that would make it even more difficult for us to be friends.

"Why not?"

The fact that he beat me up for no reason yesterday was perhaps the most significant evidence. I open my mouth to tell her this but then pause. If I tell her Colin beat me up yesterday, it'll make me look weak. I can't show weakness. I need to keep Stephanie thinking that I'm the strong man and Colin is a tool. Yet, if I tell her what happened yesterday, she'll probably be turned off by both of us.

"Well?" she asks, incensed, her hands on her hips. Man, she is so sexy when she's angry.

"I ..."

Then Martin and Colin enter the room. Colin has a punnet of grapes and a bunch of flowers. Martin stares at me for a long time. I can't read from his face what he thinks of me. I can tell that somehow Colin is holding back a smile. I would have let my temper get the better of me if Stephanie wasn't in the room.

"Are those for Stephanie or me?" I ask him.

Colin hesitates for a moment, turns to Stephanie, then me.

"They're for you, Niall. We've all been worried about you and were so glad the nurse got to you in time."

He goes to my bedside and leaves the grapes and flowers

MANIC

on top of the bedside cupboard. When his face is out of view of Stephanie's, he grins at me.

"It's a shame that the nurse found you, wee runt," he whispers, then says to the whole room, "Niall needs a bit more space. Martin, how about we play a game of table tennis?"

Martin shakes his head. "Actually, I'd like to have a word with Niall in private."

"Aww, how romantic," Colin says.

"Shut up," I roar.

Both Stephanie and Colin leave, and Martin watches them go. When the door closes, he turns to me and sighs. There is a long awkward silence until I break it.

"How are you?" I ask.

"Fine," he says unconvincingly. "What happened?"

"Colin beat me up and after, I wanted to end it all."

"I know this is a bit of a weird question but how did you … you know … do it?"

I'm slightly perplexed by Martin's question. "A blunt table knife."

"Really?"

"An exceptionally blunt table knife," I laugh, allowing a bit of black humour to get the better of me. "Trust me, a noose would be a better idea but where are you going to get a noose in a hospital?" I laugh again while Martin seems to force a grin.

"Thankfully, you're still with us."

"Yeah."

"Niall, there has been something on my mind. I …"

I jump when the door slams open against the wall. Mum, Dad and Niamh rush over to my bedside. Martin sighs and leaves the room.

"What are you playing at, son, trying to kill yourself? You've had your mother and I sick with worry. What was going on in that head of yours? Here, you certainly need this."

He throws a book onto my chest. I picked it up and looked at the cover, *The Early History of Rome* by Livy. I sigh. Oh, come on, Dad. Not another book. I haven't even looked at the other two you suggested.

"Daniel, do you think he really needs to read that now?" Mum asks.

"Of course. As Niall knows, Livy argues the study of history is the best medicine for a sick mind."

"Well, we certainly could be more considerate about Niall's current mental health."

"I've said it time and time again, reading the classics and a rake and shovel are all Niall needs to get better."

Here we go again. Dad sounds like someone scraping a polystyrene cup. I guess, in his eyes, he thinks he is doing what's best for me. But I mean, reading the classics and farm work. I've just tried to complete suicide – how are these things meant to help me?

"Look, son, we are worried about you. We've done everything we can for you to give you a good life, and then you try and throw it all away."

Mum places her hand on Dad's shoulder. "Daniel, we need to hear what the doctor and nurses think about what Niall did, rather than jumping to conclusions. Why don't you go out to the staff base? They might have something else to say. Niamh and I will talk to Niall."

Dad, still out of breath, tries to regain his composure, nods, then leaves.

Mum moves closer to my side while Niamh takes a seat by the end of the bed. "Now, Niall, your sister and I are a bit more patient than your dad. Can you tell us everything that happened and why you did what you did?"

Suddenly, the pain in my arm reminds me of why I slit my wrist. I have an eerie feeling inside me. I know why but don't want to tell her. Is it anxiety or depression? I'm not quite sure what the difference is. I give them all the details. They gasp and shake their heads as I retell everything. Then Dad opens the door and nods at Mum which makes her leave so that I'm left with Niamh. I relax and fall into my mattress more, letting out a sigh. I even close my eyes, hoping she'll let me go to sleep. I'm not that fortunate.

"How are you right now?"

It's a question that I can't answer quickly. Is there even an answer because this eerie feeling persists, but I'm more at peace than I was. I must have had a strange, melancholy face because Niamh's mouth and eyes are wide open with concern.

MANIC

"I'm better."

"Good. Now breathe. Breathe to distract yourself. Breathe in and then out slowly. You can do that?"

I take a deep breath and allow my lungs to fill up so much that my chest rises, then slowly I let it fall and I breathe out again.

"There you go. That wasn't too hard?"

I nod. But this isn't exactly going to solve all my problems.

"Keep doing that a few times and it'll help you relax. When we get stressed or anxious, we don't breathe properly. We sometimes need to make a conscious effort to breathe the right way."

I continue, in and out until I'm more relaxed on the bed.

"Now, Niall, I'm no counsellor, but I find if something is bothering me, I like to write it out in a journal."

I already knew this. I once came across one of her journals when she was young and found out she fancied Ciaran Finnegan at school.

"I don't want anybody knowing how I feel," I say.

"And that's precisely the problem we are facing right now. You thought you couldn't open up to anybody, so you felt the only way out was taking your life. What I'm suggesting with journaling is, you can at least open up to yourself and have a clearer view of your own emotions."

"I just don't want people reading ..."

"Look, set up a Google Drive account. That way nobody will ever read it unless you want them to."

That does make a lot of sense. I never knew my sister was so smart.

"Now, there is one thing I want to do with you. It's therapeutic, especially when you've gone through something traumatic. You write whatever it is that's bothering you on a sheet of paper, and once it's down, you dispose of it."

"What if somebody finds it and reads it?"

"That's where my lighter comes in handy. I'm going to go out for a smoke which will be nearly fifteen or twenty minutes. In the meantime, I want you to write down the thing that's bothering you the most."

It may come as a surprise to her that the thing that is

bothering me the most is the fact that I still have feelings for Stephanie. Stephanie wants a poem about us as just friends; I want to write a poem about us as something more.

"So, have you thought about what you're going to write?"

"Yes."

"Good, get cracking while I'm away. When I get back, I'll burn it, and you'll watch whatever's bothering you go up in flames. Trust me, you'll feel a hundred times better doing this. It works for me every time."

She sets a pen and a piece of paper on my lap and then takes out the paper for her cigarette. She puts the filter to one side of it and then tobacco on the other. She licks the end and rolls it up. She smiles at me, leaves, and gently closes the door.

Here I am, entirely on my own, with a great sense of loathing. So, what's bothering me? I can't be with Stephanie. I write the feelings I have for her, and the emotions we could have had in the future, all in the form of a poem I'm proud of, even though it's utterly worthless.

Our love
Our love together burns and is expressed
not by perfume or great expensive gifts
but by commitment and true loyalty,
with friendship being our adhesive bond.
Not like lightning that flashes in an instant
our love is like the beating of a heart.
Young love runs like a quick and shallow stream,
our love is a running river, slow but deep.
Some may strive after nymphs and angels
but we treasure what is tangible and real.
I publicly declare to all our love
but privately we show it to ourselves.
Our love's an arrow that has found its mark
but cupid never had his way with us
nor did Jupiter or Neptune conspire
our love was decreed by Almighty God.

Niamh comes back with a strong smell of tobacco, making an unusual odour with her perfume.

"How did you get on?"

"Fine."

MANIC

"Now the fun bit. Scrunch up the paper into a ball. I'll light it up, and all your problems will disappear."

I do as my sister says. She takes the paper ball and picks up the lighter. She presses down on the lighter several times with her thumb until she gets a flame. I watch the paper burn. I'm not just watching the page burn but I feel any hopes of going out with Stephanie burn up as well.

When the ball is nearly reduced to ash, Niamh turns the tap on and drops it into the sink. When the flames are extinguished, she places the ashes into the bin and turns to me.

"Now, doesn't that make you feel so much better?"

"Yes," I lie.

16

EXODUS

Friday 17th January

Two **weeks pass, and I** make a remarkable recovery from my suicide attempt. Today is the day I'll finally be leaving the hospital, hopefully for good. I've got Stephanie's number but haven't chatted to her on WhatsApp yet. I think it's best not to get in touch with her right away.

I fold the last of my clothes into my bag and I take one last look around my room – under the bed, in cupboards and under the desk – to check I've got everything. I stride confidently along the corridor to the canteen. Most of the other patients are already here, tucking into their breakfast. I take a seat with Martin. I shovel in as many spoonfuls of porridge as my mouth allows. Then I slow down and talk to Colin, who is also at our table.

MANIC

"I don't know if you already know, I'm leaving today."

"No need to rub it in."

"If we switched places, I know you'd do the same," I say.

"Probably. Thankfully, I'm not in your place."

I clench my fist, realising this is a reference to the fact he's going out with Stephanie. I take a deep breath and release it. I turn to Martin and tell him the news.

"That's great," he says. His head is bowed as he plays with his food. I try catching his eye.

"We should keep in touch."

He nods.

"Hey, I remembered there, you wanted to say something the day I awoke after my suicide attempt. What was it?"

"Oh, nothing."

A nurse walks over to me. "Niall? Could you please come with me to the medication room?"

I push my chair back and follow the nurse around the corner into the foyer. We stand outside the door of the medication room while she opens it with her keys. Previously, they weighed me here and took my blood two days prior, to check if the lithium levels in my blood were at a therapeutic level. The results came back and they're fine. Now, I'm to receive a depot injection, and I'm slightly apprehensive. What if they give me an incorrect dosage? Or what if something goes wrong and it undermines all my progress, making me the couch potato I've always feared of becoming. That's not going to make me an attractive prospect to Stephanie.

The nurse makes me stand in front of a cupboard.

"Now, Niall. What I want you to do is ever so slightly lower your trousers so we can inject your right hip."

I follow the instructions.

"Now, this should only be a little scratch," she says.

It isn't. It's a horrible sharp pain in the top of my right buttock. I clench my thigh to try to maintain my composure.

"Now, there we go. That wasn't so bad, was it?"

"No."

The nurse puts the used needle and syringe into the clinic waste bin before rubbing the wound with a cotton bud. Then she administers a plaster.

MARK BROWNLEE

"Now, you can let your mum know when you'll be needing a lift. In the meantime, you can wait in the TV room so we can check and see if you are okay."

"Fine," I say.

I watch music and news channels on TV. On the news, China is making manoeuvres around the coast of Taiwan. In Europe, Russia continues to interfere with the internal affairs of Ukraine. The news coverage includes a short response from President Edwards. He promises to defend the people of Ukraine and Taiwan.

When the story ends, I change the TV to a music channel where Ed Sheeran sings *Perfect*. Stephanie said she liked him. It's hard to listen to it without feeling emotional. It's as if Sheeran had written the song for Stephanie and me.

The nurse comes in with some paperwork for me to sign; I do so with my illegible scribble. I make my way along to my room to collect my bag. As I leave, I slam the door and run along the corridor screaming, "I'm going home! I'm going home!"

Doctor Henson stands talking to my mum. He turns and smiles. "If you start acting like that, we'll have to reconsider keeping you here."

"Are you ready?" Mum asks.

"Hang on. I want to say one last goodbye."

"Hey, Colin. You don't know where Martin is?"

"He's in his room."

I try to find him but he is nowhere to be seen. Why isn't he here to see me off? It seems rather weird.

I meet Mum and then we leave together. I'm free! As I stand in the dry winter's day, I pause with eyes closed, and breathe in the cold refreshing air before following Mum to the car.

I ponder as we make our way into Armagh and the spires of the cathedrals cut the skyline. Is there something I can do now that I'm out of hospital to impress Stephanie? I remember she said she would like to be a lecturer one day. What if she became a lecturer in my university, the University of Armagh? It's a great idea. After all, Armagh is called the place of saints and scholars. How could a place of scholars not have a

MANIC

university in this day and age? I wish I could be with her in Bangor. I could build a railway line from Armagh to Portadown so I could go to her any time I wanted, without any need to depend on Mum or Dad to give me a lift. But could I really achieve all this?

I unfasten my seatbelt and leave the vehicle. It's raining, so I pull up the hood of my jumper and walk across the car park to the shopping centre.

I loiter, not interested in going into any of the shops. There's a crane machine full of toys. I never usually play with these machines. The gadgets remind me of my episode in the hospital when everyone had a familiar on their shoulder except me. The machine says you need fifty pence to have one go and a pound for three goes. I will probably need several goes, so I insert a pound. Passers-by look over as the machine lights up with a loud comical noise.

There's a toy turtle that catches my eye. I move my claw down towards its head and press the button that closes the claw around it. I manage to lift it ever so slightly up then drop it. The second time, I manage to raise it and bring it over to the drop that leads to the opening, but the toy falls before it reaches the drop. On my last go, I lift the toy by the torso, raise it above the edge of the slide and let it go so it falls to the opening. I put my hand in past the flap and grab my newly acquired toy. I hold it and stare at it. The turtle is an apt familiar for myself. After all, I was always a good swimmer like the turtle, and perhaps more interestingly, I spend a lot of my time and space in my shell. I decide to call him, Teddy the turtle.

I take the new toy and help Mum bag groceries at the checkout in the supermarket. When I finish, I watch her insert a credit card into the machine. What things could I buy with it? Something I couldn't do since my debit card was cancelled. She puts her card back into her purse. If only I could get my hands on it, I could buy whatever I want. When we arrive home, her phone sounds with a loud ring tone that would give you a fright if you weren't used to it. She opens her handbag, rummaging around it until she finds the device. She answers and leaves the room. Now that she's gone, I go over to her handbag and try to

MARK BROWNLEE

find her purse, which proves more difficult than I thought. Mum's voice in the hallway is getting nearer and then farther away as she walks back and forth past the door.

I find the purse where there are all kinds of things: receipts, cards, change. Where is her credit card? I can't find it. Her voice is growing nearer and the fact she is saying "bye" means I've only seconds before she's back in the room. Finally, I find it and grab it before zipping up the purse and putting it back into her handbag. She comes back, unsuspecting and smiling.

"Niall, I have to say you're a good son helping me put the groceries away. Do you know what? You deserve some pocket money."

"No, Mum. I'm fine."

"I insist. You've come out of the hospital; we need to celebrate that fact."

She opens her handbag and purse and hands me a twenty-pound note. I take it, saying thanks. With Mum's card in my pocket, I go to my room and then onto my laptop where I do some online shopping. First, I make purchases in line with my ambition to set up a university: an academic gown and cap costing a total of two hundred pounds; some academic history books that will help me get a degree – another one hundred pounds; the works of the metaphysical poets to impress Stephanie – seventy pounds. For more leisurely purposes, I spend excessively. In total, one thousand, four hundred and twenty-one pounds is spent in half an hour.

What if James Edwards came to the inauguration service of my university? Then I remember the letter I wrote and gave to Conor to send. I had totally forgotten about that. I need to know if he sent it So I run out into the farm and find him.

"Conor! Conor! Did you send the letter?"

He stands in one of the sheds moving bales. He stops and rubs bits of straw from his overalls.

"Sorry, Niall. I forgot."

My jaw drops. "You forgot?"

"Here, it's still in my coat pocket."

He takes the letter, all scrunched up, and hands it to me.

I immediately put the letter in the postbox near the end

MANIC

of our lane. Now it's only a matter of time before Edwards will be paying a visit to Ireland and, more importantly, my home. I need to get in touch with Stephanie. I go onto my Messenger account and start talking to her. She stays online.

-Hey, friend. How are you keeping?

She replies immediately.

-Fine. You?

-Grand. I remember you said you would like to be a lecturer one day. I can help you out.

-Why, do you know somebody who could give me a generous scholarship to a world-renowned university?

-No, I plan to set up a world-renowned university in Armagh, where you can be a lecturer, like myself.

-Sounds like a great idea, Niall. But who is going to fund all this?

-Money is no obstacle.

-I know it isn't, but it's the thing that helps you to get over the obstacle.

-What about a commune on my dad's farm?

-A commune? Yes, that might work. Niall, are you sure everything's okay?

-Yes, why wouldn't it be?

-You've just shared very unrealistic goals to me. I wonder if you're okay.

-I'm fine, Stephanie. Really, I've never felt better.

17

LOSING IT

Saturday 1st February

I t's now **February, two weeks** since I left the hospital. Mum went mental when she found out how much money I'd spent on her card but she has mellowed since then. The home treatment team come and see me every few days. If it weren't for Dad, I probably wouldn't need them. Today is his birthday.

I sit at the desk in my room with intentions of doing some reading. I recently read *Sophie's World* which was a good introduction to philosophy and made me confident enough to dive into the actual works of the famous philosophers. I read bits of Soren Kierkagaard's *Fear and Trembling* and George Berkeley's *A Treatise Concerning the Principles of Human Knowledge*. It didn't take me long to realise I'm totally out of my depth. I turn to the last page I was reading and remove the

MANIC

bookmark.

I hear my dad sigh from his room next door and fumble as he changes out of his work clothes. Then he walks into my room.

"What are you reading?" he asks, looking over my shoulder.

I close the book and hide the cover from his sight, knowing he won't approve.

"What's that? Kierkegaard? And Berkeley? Niall, I've told you before and I'll say it again, the darkest time in Western Civilization wasn't the Dark Ages but the Enlightenment. I mean, you can't seriously believe Berkeley's argument that things only exist if they are experienced. And Kierkegaard's pathetic idea of a leap of faith. I taught you to think, not to feel. Faith should not be a leap; it should always be based on reason. Have a look at Aquinas' Five Ways or, in my opinion, the strongest argument for the existence of God, Anselm's Ontological Argument."

In my opinion, I always thought the Ontological Argument was the weakest argument for the existence of God but that's just me.

"What is it?" Dad asks as we all wait for him to open a present.

"You're only going to find out if you open it," Mum says, trying to keep her voice light. She's struggling to look at him. Both her hands are clutching at each other as her fingers fidget.

He fumbles at the large, wrapped box with a frown on his face. He unwraps the fold of paper then he reveals to everyone a power drill.

"How did you know?" he asks in astonishment.

Conor conjures up a fake smile. "We all knew. You've been mad about that for the past year."

He laughs awkwardly as Dad removes the device from the box and pretends to use it.

There's a chocolate cake on the table that Mum has made. We all sit with hesitation as Mum brings over plates. Conor takes a giant knife and cuts the cake into eighths with some reservation.

134

After the empty festivities, I go back to my room and decide to read a book that is more accessible than Kierkegaard or Berkeley. My favourite author and my favourite book: *God Exists* by James Edwards. As I casually flick through the pages, a question arises in my head: am I crazy? Only a little. Maybe I don't need the home treatment team. I can cure myself by reasoning my way out of insanity. I will engage my mind with the many rational arguments for the existence of God in Edwards' book. Such activity will cure me of my partial insanity.

I read the book from where I left off until the elven queen Galadriel speaks to me.

Greetings, Tom Bombadil of the forest. What you are currently doing may seem wise, yet another approach may be required. You are a colossus and will achieve great things. You are one who will change the course of history.

"How? I'm going mad."

In time, your mind will heal.

"How will I change the course of history?" I say aloud.

By saving the world from destruction. You will require a mentor to tap your greatness.

"A mentor? Who? Edwards?"

The one you speak of will come, and you will learn from him. You will be his prodigy, and you will outgrow him in greatness.

I laugh and jump up and down. Edwards will be my mentor, and he will teach me everything he knows. When will I meet him? I pause to think of an answer. He will come and meet me today in my home. I need to be ready and tidy my room. I shake. I'm about to meet my hero. What if I'm speechless? Will I be able to contain my excitement and keep my composure when he arrives? I can't at the mere prospect of it.

I clutch my crucifix and pray to the Virgin Mary.

Fear not, child. For the angels of Heaven hold you in high esteem. Fear not the stature of other men for all come and go to dust. So will you but your spirit shall be spared decay. Do not fear your present illness for you will experience healing. You have a bright future ahead of you where you will save many by your great deeds.

MANIC

I'm enthralled by the queen of Heaven in all her glory and splendour. She wears a white linen gown that shines like the moon. Her dark hair flows down either side of her face and rests on her shoulders. On her head is a crown of pearls that dangles over the brow of her cream face which glows rays of light. Her brown eyes are filled with compassion and relieve me of all my fears. More comfort comes when the mother of God kneels down, places her hands together and closes her eyes.

I will be praying for you.

I'm emotional. I've had a religious experience, one far greater than any other I have ever had before. Such an experience can never leave a person unchanged. It could take me on a new course in my life. I could become a monk or a priest. I can save many by my great deeds in that occupation but the vow of chastity puts me off the idea. For I long to be with Stephanie more. To talk to her, to merely be with her. Then the goddess Venus speaks.

Niall, you are to be the saviour of the world, not a humble priest but a great general who will conquer nations. Take Stephanie as your lover. She will acknowledge your true greatness.

With all these voices, it's clear that my family will think I'm unwell and readmit me to hospital. I have to find a solution. Have I not already got one? Reason? Yet it requires a lot of concentration to read Edwards' book with all these voices speaking. I open the book again to the last page I was reading and hope there will be no further distraction. Then there's a knock at the door.

"It's Niamh. Are you decent?"

"Yeah."

She opens the door and stares at me with my book open. "What are you reading?"

"*God Exists* by James Edwards."

"You know, Niall, for a Catholic you've a strange fascination for that Protestant minister." She should speak for herself, always dabbling in different religions. She's only Catholic when it suits her.

"He's the most powerful man in the world. Know your enemy so you can make him your friend."

136

MARK BROWNLEE

"Who said that?"

"Sun Tzu," I say. Well, at least the enemy bit. I made up the bit about making him your friend though."

"I thought I'd check up on you. I'm heading out now. Can you hold the fort?"

"Sure."

I decide to read an author other than Edwards. Rummaging through my bookshelves, *Orthodoxy* by G.K. Chesterton catches my eye. It's undoubtedly logical in its content and would help me reason my way out of psychosis. I open the book, turn to the contents page and notice that chapter two is entitled 'the maniac'.

I remember reading this chapter, but I can't remember what Chesterton said made people manic. I find out that the overuse of reason leads to madness while imagination cures it. Hang on. That's the complete opposite of what I've been doing. He argues creativity tries only to express a part of reality while reason seeks to contain it all in one's head, and the head cracks as a result. Great, all I have to do is imagine things with my brain. I need the freedom of the outside world to allow my imagination to go wild.

I tiptoe out of my room. The kitchen door is shut. Niamh might still be in. if I can pass the door quietly and open and close the front door without any noise, I'll be a free man. I turn the corner and something stops me dead in my tracks. It's my old lightsabre from when I was a kid lying on the floor. I pick it up then dash towards the front door and clumsily open it before sprinting along the garden path and then the farm lane.

I stand halfway down the lane where the narrow stream marks the edge of Dad's orchards. I go into it and put on my earphones to play some music. With my lightsabre turned on, I wave it, causing it to make a 'vroom, vroom' sound effect. I'm ready to test G.K. Chesterton's thesis that imagination can cure madness. I take out my phone and put Spotify on shuffle. A track by Alanis Morrissette called *All I Really Want* strikes me. All I really want is Stephanie and to be sane, for I need to be sane to get her. I play the track and listen to the lyrics Then I take my jumper off and put it inside out and around backwards. I proceed to jump up and down again and again. This whole

MANIC

psychosis thing is nothing more than a cloud hanging over me. The track *Wake up* by Rage Against the Machine plays. I need to wake up from my psychosis. I move through the orchard out onto the road. I run along the lane with my lightsabre like a fast-flowing river. I turn to a field full of cattle. Nine Ringwraiths threaten me with their blades. I laugh. I'm Tom Bombadil. I don't possess the ring. I shout, scare and intimidate them with my glowing lightsabre.

Taylor Swift's hit *Shake it Off* comes on. That's all I have to do. Shake it off. Shake off my psychosis, madness, mania and insanity in a simple feel-good, carefree motion. So, I dance throughout her track and at times even try to shake every part of my body physically. And I'm saner now than I've ever been.

Maybe it's now best to head home. I walk back at a perfectly normal pace, dragging my lightsabre behind me. I'm experiencing a lull. Does that mean I'm now sane? Then the Almighty speaks to me. *Beloved child, I will give you the strength to become a mighty warrior and leader of men to fulfil my great purposes on earth.*

I immediately respond. "Lord, I'm willing to die for You, the same way You died for me."

I'm sure once I get back home, Edwards will be there to meet me. I march up the lane. I imagine that my family and Edwards are singing the Civil War song, *Johnny Comes Marching Home,* only it's me marching home. I smile as I listen to the lyrics played out in my head.

Soon, I'm in front of my home again. I move up the front driveway and around the side, past the clothesline to the back of the house. I enter and pass through the utility room into the kitchen, where I hope my whole family will be. Over by the door into the hallway, my face lights up. A casually dressed man smiles at me and I smile back.

"Mr Edwards, it's a great pleasure to meet you. Please, make yourself at home."

18

MR EDWARDS

Saturday 1st February

Edwards stands in the kitchen by the dining room table. He glances over at the dirty dishes in the sink and smiles. He's certainly not how I imagined him. He's slim with dark hair with hints of grey. They always say famous people seem smaller than how you perceive them in the media. I'm speechless at the fact I'm able to meet him in the flesh, up close and personal. He laughs when I gasp at his presence.

"You must be Niall Alexander, or should I call you Tom Bombadil?"

"How do you know?" I say, shocked at his awareness.

He grins. "I got your letter. You're probably wondering why I'm here?"

I nod.

MANIC

He turns his head to his left and then to the right to make absolutely certain we are the only two people in the room.

"Do you promise to keep a secret?"

"Of course."

"In your letter, you said I was Théoden, king of Rohan. You probably know he comes to the aid of Gondor, after dealing with the threat of Isengard in the west. There is a growing threat now in both the West and East."

I gulp, trying to keep down my portion of Dad's birthday cake. "China and Russia."

He nods. "Yes, World War Four will soon break out, and it's my responsibility in office to prepare those who will come after me to be ready for it."

I frown at this and scratch the top of my head. "World War Four? Hang on, World War Three hasn't even taken place. What are you talking about?"

"Oh, come on, Niall. World War One saw Germany defeated but still able to recover and seek revenge in World War Two when they experienced total defeat. World War Three, also known as the Cold War, saw the defeated power Russia humiliated but able to recover and now seek revenge. World War Four will end up being more destructive than all the previous ones."

Still frowning, I tilt my head to the right and fold my arms. "Surely nuclear weapons mean people are too scared of acting in ways that would cause another world war."

He smiles. "You're talking about mutually assured nuclear destruction. What if I was to tell you that was a load of garbage?"

I crinkle my nose. "Is it?"

"Have you ever heard of the Star Wars program, Niall?"

I raise my chin. "That was something when Reagan was President."

"That's right. It's the idea that nuclear missiles can be shot out of the sky before they meet their target. Ourselves, Russia and China have our defence programs that make ballistic nuclear weapons redundant. Yet I've always been a firm believer in nuclear peace theory. Now I envisage the mass mobilisation and conscription of people to fight, and this time

140

MARK BROWNLEE

the body count will be much greater than World War Two."

"Why are you telling me all this, especially since it's top secret?"

Edwards pauses for a moment without taking his gaze off me. "Because you are my successor."

My mouth drops and I unfold my arms and put them up in a defensive pose. "No, no. I'm no politician."

"The successor who I hope will carry on my legacy isn't a politician but a military man. Someone who can succeed where Hitler and Napoleon failed, and conquer Russia."

My jaw drops and I'm flabbergasted by what he has just said. I'm flattered that he thinks I'll be a general someday. Yet surely there must be someone else. Why me? I haven't even got my A-Levels yet.

He leans his head closer into my personal space. "I've foreseen it. I had a vision last month of you standing in triumph in Moscow. Then the Lord guided me to your home, and that's why I'm here now. Niall, you are God's chosen one who will spread democracy to the ends of the earth."

I don't know what to say. It does all seem rather far-fetched. But I honestly believe that the man standing before me is the POTUS.

"This is all well and good, Mr Edwards, but why are you telling me all of this now? When I'm stressed. I've just got out of the hospital. To be honest, I'd much rather snog Stephanie than save the world by conquering Russia."

"Niall, you're the one God has chosen for this task. In regard to Stephanie, you are the Irish revolutionary, Michael Collins. It was his military and political success that got him the beautiful Kitty Kiernan. Be who you were born to be. Embrace your God-given genius, and you'll find you'll turn Stephanie's head by doing it."

A car drives up the lane and I run to the window. It's Mum, back from the supermarket. I turn around to Edwards, ready to tell him to hide. But he's gone.

What does this all mean? Would I one day be called Niall Alexander the Great? To such an extent that when somebody mentions Alexander the Great, they'll have to clarify which one. Yet, despite everything, my desire for Stephanie remains the

MANIC

same. What's the point of saving the world if you've got nobody to save it for? I want Stephanie, and if I have to conquer the whole world to get her, then I will gladly do it.

Mum comes into the room with two large shopping bags and with her sunglasses on.

"You alright? You look as pale as milk," she says.

"Oh, it's nothing. Let me help you with the groceries."

I put the items away as someone outside mutters. It's Dad staggering across the driveway with a whiskey bottle. He's been like this before; it's a common occurrence that never ends well. I nudge Mum and point at him. Her face falls as she puts some yoghurts in the fridge.

"Mum, you need to leave. You know what this is going to go on to."

"No, you have to face your fears. Who knows, we might be able to reason with him."

There's no chance and Mum knows it. I can never tell what keeps her with Dad. If I was in her shoes, I would have left him long ago.

He opens the door and falls onto the floor of the utility room, spilling whiskey everywhere. He manages to pick himself up, laughing.

"Hello, you lovely people. I'm feeling fantastic."

"Daniel, you've had a little too much," Mum says, putting the last of the groceries away.

Dad frowns and points his finger at eye level. "Don't you tell me when I've had too much, or you'll know about it."

"Is that a threat?" I ask. Wow, that just slipped out. Come on, Niall, step up and grow a set.

"Don't you get involved in this, Niall. It's between me and your mother."

My entire body suddenly stiffens. "You can't treat her like dirt."

"I can treat her anyway I want. She's my wife."

"You may find one day she'll have had enough and leave."

Mum stares at me. Dad glares at her. We all know she never will. I want to say something or do something that will stop the beatings, but I can't do anything.

"Niall," Dad says, "go to your room. This doesn't concern

you."

It involves both my parents, so it certainly does concern me. I remember what Mr Edwards said to me about embracing my God-given genius. I do something I've never done before. Stand up to my dad and assert myself.

"No. I will not go to my room."

"What? I'm telling you to go to your room, so you obey, or you'll feel my fist in your face."

"No, I will not go, and if you assault Mum or me, I'm going to call the police."

"Niall, you won't do such a thing. You're too proud."

What does he mean by proud?

"You don't want people to know about this for the same reason I don't. It looks bad. Everyone sees us, the Alexanders are a nice, respectful family. Do you want that to end?"

"I want this abuse to end, and if I disgrace the family name in the process, I don't care."

Dad slowly walks over to me with a raised hand and hits my left cheek so hard I fall onto the floor. I'm big but he's bigger. He stands over me as I get up. When our gaze meets, there's only hatred in his eyes.

"Go to your room, now."

I leave, dejected, and sit in the corner of my bedroom clutching my shins, crying my eyes out at all the noise in the kitchen. The thumps, the cries and the screeches then the silence, sounding worse than the noise. I take out my phone, and I'm about to dial nine-nine-nine, when suddenly my bedroom door is thrown open. Dad marches in and grabs the device.

"So, you were going to ring the police. We can't have that," he laughs. "If you ever do such a thing ever again, I'll turn you and your mum into a pulp. Do you understand?"

I nod, shaking.

"Good."

Later, when Dad isn't looking, I find a phone. Should I ring the police? If he finds out, he'll only give me another hiding but I can't let Dad continue to do the things he does. I shake as I hold the device. Can I do this? I dial nine-nine-nine like before

MANIC

and when the operator speaks back to me, I'm careful not to talk too loudly so Dad doesn't hear me. I tell her the situation to which she replies that a police car will be sent immediately to the house to assess the situation.

When I hang up, I break down. How am I ever going to be the great general Edwards talked about if I can't assert myself in my own home. I'm such a weakling that I can't protect my mum.

I sit in my room beside my bookshelf and glance at the titles to see if any catch my eye. James Edwards' bestseller *God Exists* towers above the rest, I flick through it again. Edwards puts forward the arguments for the existence of God in it and then addresses those arguments against it. I knew which one was the most persuasive against the presence of God: evil. How can a God of love allow evil and suffering? I read his response and it reminds me that Christians believe that God lived and died as a human being and so understands what it's like to suffer. For all I know, Stephanie is suffering right now with something. I realise suffering can be a strength, not just a weakness.

19

AKATHISIA

Saturday 1ˢᵗ February –

Sunday 16ᵗʰ February

message Stephanie in the hope that I can be there for her.

-I'd like to meet up with you at some point tomorrow.

Her reply comes almost immediately.

-I'm busy most of this week and next. I'm trying to catch up with schoolwork. How about Saturday fortnight? You can pop down to Bangor.

-Cool, I'll see you then.

I watch the police car drive into the farmyard. Red-faced and sweaty, Dad goes out. The two male officers chat with him for a while; I can't hear what they're saying even when I open the window. Then, all three of them walk in the direction of the house. An officer stares at me when he enters.

"So, you're the person who rang to say your dad assaulted your mum."

I nod.

"Your father says he didn't."

"He's the boy who cries wolf," Dad says.

"Where is your mother?" the other police officer asks.

"She's at her sister's," Dad says.

"Yeah, because you nearly killed her," I yell, hoping that he'll lose his composure. "Ring her to get her side of the story. Here, you can use our telephone."

Dad hesitantly points them to our house phone in the utility room.

I watch and wait as one of the officers talks over the phone. After several minutes, he comes into the kitchen.

"Your mother says that she was not assaulted tonight and that she's fine."

Dad gasps. "See," he says. "It's a shame my son has to waste precious police time. I hope he learns his lesson about lying."

"I'm not lying."

"My son hasn't been feeling the best of late; he's only recently come out of a psychiatric hospital. That probably explains all the strange ideas he's been having."

The police glance at each other then nod at Dad.

"No," I say. "He is lying to you about Mum. He assaulted her."

"Your mum said he didn't. We would only be able to press charges against your father if your mum comes forward."

Adrenaline spikes inside me and I hear blood rush in my ears. Why didn't Mum do that? After they have a few more words with Dad, the police officers leave. Dad walks them to their car. He waves them off as the car speeds away on the gravel.

Dad closes the door behind him and he turns and rests his back against it. He smiles at me as he slowly slides his back against the wooden surface.

"So, you thought you could get me into trouble. The only person who's in trouble now is you."

He runs towards me, hand raised and fists clenched and punches me in the eye. I recoil back slightly but don't fall over. I press my hand where it's sore. Both my eyes water and I'm in a daze as my stomach hardens.

"Let that be a lesson to you. I don't want you sitting about doing nothing. You need to do some work on the farm like your older brother. If you don't work, I'll give you another black eye."

I know being physically assaulted by anybody is a big deal and even more so when it's your dad. There's that sense of betrayal from the very people you should expect and depend on to love and care for you. But the more often it happens, the more you ask yourself, will this be the norm? I'm frightened of even considering the idea that it might already be the norm and there's nothing I can do about it. I'm not there yet but how long will it take for the abuse to grind me to the point that I accept it and do nothing about it?

The next morning, I get my breakfast and put on some boots, overalls, a coat, and a woolly hat. I look at the dirty mirror above the sink and sigh. Will I be able to get through this day?

Limping slightly as I have a cramp in my leg, I walk across the yard to where Conor comes out of the milking parlour with two buckets of milk. He comes towards me with a frown.

"Hey, what happened to your eye?"

I frown, knowing that if he guesses he'll probably get the right answer.

"You're up early," he continues.

"Dad said I should do a bit more work on the farm."

"I've got most of it covered. Dad's milking while I'm doing everything else. You could do some dung scraping – the little corner in the old cattle shed – with the hand scraper. I've already scraped the rest with the tractor."

It isn't exactly the most attractive sort of work to be doing, but I reluctantly agree. I work in an ungrated area in the shed, scraping all the dung to the grated area, where it leaks

MANIC

down into the tank below. The stench is absolutely revolting, just a nice reminder that my life right now isn't just crap. It's literally in the crap as well. Will things ever change?

When I finish, I enter the milking parlour where Dad is. We say nothing, standing in the trench between the cows elevated on either side. He continually snakes through the glass containers that hang in the middle of the channel and puts the clusters on the cows' udders. When all the clusters are on, he pauses and frowns at me. He's waiting silently for Conor to return. When he does, he places the two empty buckets beside the valve where he can get milk for feeding.

He turns to me. "You finished?"

"Yeah."

"That's you. I've got everything else covered. How about you take it easy, at least for today?" Conor says.

"I don't want him being idle," Dad says.

You've always ensured that I'll never be idle. The beatings always terrify me into working more. Thankfully, Conor always covers my back, helping with tasks I can't do or am too busy to do because of schoolwork.

"Don't worry, Dad. I'll do all the work you had in mind for him."

I nod, kind of glad because he was probably only going to give me the crap jobs anyway.

"Mum said you've still got a bit more time to recover. The home treatment team will be coming out to check up on you. Hopefully, you'll make the progress they desire. Then you'll be able to work more with us on the farm if you want. Okay?" Conor says.

"Okay," I say.

Leaving the milking parlour, I walk across to the middle of the yard then down the lane, the same route I so often take around the country roads near my house. Snow lies on the ground. There is a cold northerly breeze that blows against me as I walk but it doesn't deter me. There is an orchard on each side of me. There is a deadness to each tree, a condition to be expected at this time of year. I shiver; my teeth rattle in the cold and my breath forms a cloud when I breathe.

I continue turning right and walk farther down the road

MARK BROWNLEE

with white fields on each side of me. I ascend a hill and see my home in the west and the spires of the cathedral of Armagh in the south so I bless myself. I find my way onto the back lane of the farm. In comparison to the front lane, it desperately needs some urgent resurfacing, something Dad has never addressed. For all of Dad's talk of civilization, you'd think he would keep this place in better shape. Granted, it will never be Rome but it could be something more if he tried.

When I return, there is a car in the driveway that I don't recognise. I enter the house to find two female nurses sitting on the sofa.

A long pause ensues before one speaks up.

"Niall, we know you've been discharged, yet we feel we need to continue to check up on you over the next few weeks to ensure you make a steady recovery and then hopefully you'll be able to go back to school."

I don't exactly want to go back to school now but have I not already recovered? What are they still concerned about?

"We want to make sure you are taking your medication, and that there aren't any side effects to the Abilify depot injection administered to you. How are you at present?"

"Great," I reply. Although that might be a bad sign to them that I am experiencing a manic episode.

"We are going to monitor your mood as well, which at the minute is stable. We'll have a chat with your parents now. Oh, and by the way, how did you get that bad bruise on your face."

So, they've put me on the spot and my immediate instinct is to tell them the truth. I open my mouth to speak and then I see Dad peering in from the kitchen doorway, shaking his head. My limbs shake and my heart races. I can't believe this is happening. That's right, folks. I'm chickening out, but can't you see I've tried before with the police and failed. How is this time going to be any different? If I tell the truth, I'll not be believed and I'll get another beating from you know who, only this time much worse. I mean, let's not kid ourselves here. If you were in the nurses' shoes, who would you believe? The psychotic teenager or the well-respected middle-class former academic. Yep, I rest my case. So no, I can't tell the truth.

I point at my eye. "What is this? Aw, Conor and I were

MANIC

messing around with a bit of play fighting that got out of hand."

"It clearly did," one of the nurses says with shock in her voice.

I leave as my parents enter. Dad smiles at me and nods. When they finish talking to my parents, they invite me back in and tell me they'll be back in a few days.

A new day comes. I rise as early as the previous one. I need to work hard on the farm today if I want to set up a commune for Stephanie. I know some might say this is an unrealistic goal but I believe I could achieve it and besides, I've got my whole life ahead of me to make it a reality. If I can impress Dad by working hard, it means I might get a share of the inheritance which I can use to set up my commune. To my amazement, I find I'm out onto the farm before Conor. I feed the calves in different locations across the farm. One area is in the yard behind the office. There are four white plastic hutches with an entrance that leads out to a small space with metal fencing. I give each calf an appropriate amount of milk and top up their water buckets while also ensuring their troughs are full of feed. I then go into the milking parlour and expect an earful from Dad. Not long after I arrive, a scruffy Conor runs in and stands above us down in the trench. Dad stares at me then Conor takes me out of the milking parlour to the yard. "Niall, take it easy for the rest of the day. I've got your back. Don't worry about Dad."

I frown then nod.

The home treatment nurses come more frequently. I sit in front of them but can't remain still. I keep shaking my legs restlessly and even get up and pace up and down either side of the room. I probably look like a right eejit to them. I have drastically increased the amount of walking I do in a day. I still limit it to walking and nothing more as excessive exercise might result in a manic episode. Yet I can't help it. There is something inside me that compels me to walk. I can't sit down to watch TV or read a book. From dawn to dusk, I walk the route around my house and extend it farther. I walk around the borders of fields and up the grassy pathways of the orchards.

Snow is on the ground and crunches as I stomp each step

MARK BROWNLEE

on my dad's land. The dead of winter and bitter chill soon comes to bite me. I'm usually suitably attired to battle the elements as when it snows heavily, it's hard to bear. A neighbour makes small talk and strangers offer to give me a lift. I refuse each time because I have to walk and have no other choice.

Day after day, I'm locked in the same torturous routine. I'm in no fit state to meet Stephanie. I want to cancel our meeting but I don't want her to know the real reason why – that I'm always walking around the countryside like some headless chicken.

I wake at dawn on the day I'm meant to meet up with Stephanie – the same time as Conor and Dad – and do the dung scraping. It's the only task I'm capable of doing at the minute. I take to walking around the house then I go inside to sit in the living room. Both legs are shaking against the sofa. It's unbearable. I try to find relief by lying on the floor but this only leads me to toss and turn. Then I walk up and down the narrow hallway, back and forth in front of its mirror, talking to myself. Then I do another walk around, the same route outside, before coming back inside to sit down with shaky legs, spend another brief time rolling on the floor and then pacing up and down the hallway. Then all again and again and then still day after day without any relief. After the hundredth cycle, I'm tossing and turning aggressively on the floor like a fish out of water. I place my forehead onto the living room carpet. I'm nauseous and there is a feeling of coldness all over me. I'm unable to draw a deep breath because I'm reflexively pushing down on my diaphragm. I break down. Tears run down my face as I cry. "God, please, let me die." The sensation of time has slowed to the movement of a slug as each millisecond picks at my brain like a pinprick.

That evening, after my last walk of the day, I limp to the chair by the door and let out a loud sigh. Niamh notices me while washing the dishes.

"Are you alright?" she asks.

"I feel like I've been through the wars. My feet are killing me."

She dries her hands and moves over to where I'm sitting.

MANIC

She helps me remove my socks which reveal two bare feet with torn skin in multiple places. She's horrified by what she sees. I'm not surprised.

There's a ping from my phone. It's Stephanie

-Hey, Niall. I thought you were coming to see me today.

I sigh. If only I could be there with her like I said. My stomach clenches. When will I ever see you again?

-Sorry. I haven't been feeling the best. I'll meet up with you soon when I'm better.

-No worries. Steph.

The next day, the nurses arrive and I can tell they're more concerned about me. Their eyes widen when I show them my feet.

I fall and plant my face into the floor. "I want to die. Please kill me!" I sob.

They say nothing. Well, that means I need to be more persuasive. I stand up and stare at the short female nurse who smiles at me. I need to get her attention. I grab her by the collar and shake her.

"Kill me. Kill me," I scream at the top of my voice as she protests, trying to get away.

The male nurse with her is bigger and taller than me and manages to restrain me. I fall to the ground.

"I'm sorry," I moan. "But there's something wrong with my feet. I can't stop walking."

The next day, the nurses are joined by a consultant named Doctor Smith. She's a slim, middle-aged woman with long blonde hair. She wears thin-rimmed glasses and a white tweed skirt and white suit jacket with black borders. She sits on the sofa in front of me, her leg crossed. No! I know what this means; they're going to chuck me back into the slammer again. She listens to me attentively as I explain my plight over the past few weeks. We talk for a while and I tell her how I feel. She nods a lot. I ask if I can get any relief. She pauses for a while before asking me to leave while she has a chat with Mum and Dad. I wait restlessly on my bed, twitching, before Dad tells me to come back into the room.

Doctor Smith turns to me. "Niall, you are suffering from akathisia."

Aka what? But there is a more pressing question to ask her. "Am I going back to the hospital?"

She shakes her head.

I let out a loud sigh and thank Saint Nick for a late Christmas present. Then I ask her the other question.

"What's akathisia?"

20

HUGS NOT DRUGS

Sunday 16th February –

Thursday 27th February

A**kathisia is a subjective feeling** of motor restlessness manifested by a compelling need to be in constant movement. It is a disorder experienced by patients who have adverse side effects to medication," Doctor Smith says, as if she is reading from a textbook. She pauses for a moment and turns to the nurses.

"It's most likely the antipsychotic depot injection administered to you in the hospital that is the cause. All we can do is wait for the effects of the injection to wear off. The home treatment team will continue to monitor you, and if your condition worsens, we'll have no choice but to readmit you to hospital."

The only thing I heard from her whole big doctor spiel was, "we'll have no choice but to readmit you to hospital." But surely if they know what's wrong with me now, they'll not have to do that. Just give me some new drugs and let the home treatment team do the rest.

"Can you give me something for this?"

She shakes her head.

I keep crossing my legs. No drug that can wipe away or relieve me of my symptoms. I'll have to wait it out? That sounds unbearable. My muscles are sore, stiff and cramping, in particular my legs. But there is some comfort in the fact that my plight has been diagnosed; it's no longer a mystery, and hopefully, in time, it'll be easier.

Each day is similar to the one before – dung scraping in the morning, numerous walks outside, brief but tortuous moments sitting down or rolling on my bed. I lie there and gaze up at the ceiling, back flat and knees bent. I manage to remain still for almost three minutes before I get up again. Some days, if I sleep in, Dad pours a jug of cold water over me in bed.

"What did you do that for?" I protest.

"What doesn't kill you makes you stronger. Friedrich Nietzsche."

I'm bored and want something to do other than the same routine of the past two weeks. Then I grin. I'll get in touch with Stephanie.

I swipe my phone and go onto WhatsApp, hoping Stephanie will be on. She's not. Will I have the courage to talk to her? What will I say to get her attention? I stare at my phone, eyes fixed on the screen.

I click her name on the chat column. It brings up the chat box that lists the last conversation I had with her. I bombard her with messages to force her to reply out of annoyance. Random songs from YouTube.

The chat box shows that she's typing a reply. My insides turn to wax. What is she going to say next?

-Hi Niall. How are you?

MANIC

A simple and perfectly legitimate question for Stephanie considering the circumstances but it is one I found impossible to answer.

-I'm fine. How are you?

-To be honest, I could be better. I've had a real bad week with anxiety but I think I've turned a corner.

I don't know what to say. In the hospital, I was the one who lived life as an open book and Stephanie was the one more guarded about her illness and personal life. I want to be able to encourage and comfort her but my own plight and feelings of hopelessness would make me something of a hypocrite.

In the end, I'm only able to pathetically type the words:

-Get well soon.

Get well soon? Sounds like a platitude off a bad greeting card.

I'm such a fool but Stephanie is all I want. No, it's moved on from 'want' to 'need'. I'm curious and go on Colin's Instagram. When I view some of his profile pictures it's clear, he loves himself and enjoys looking at his own reflection.

One day, when I take my place on the world stage and create a new world order, my first decree will be to have Colin suffer a slow and painful death. I'll be a military hero and genius to millions with history remembering me as the young man who saved the world from destruction and then Stephanie will be my girlfriend. No, my wife.

All this reminds me of Edwards, the man who told me to embrace my God-given genius. What about a phone call to him? I couldn't just simply ring up the White House, but I could ring up his former church where he was a pastor – Sixth Avenue Church of God. Edwards could help me become the saviour of the world. I ring the church from my mobile after getting the number off the internet.

"Hello, this is Sixth Avenue Church of God. Jerry speaking. How can I help you?"

"Hello, Jerry. This is Niall Alexander. Make sure this gets to the top. Tell Edwards I need his help in getting a girl but also in saving the world. I've talked to him before. If he wants to come to my home again in Ireland, he can, and there he can

156

MARK BROWNLEE

continue where we left off in our conversation."

"O-kay," Jerry says. "James Edwards is no longer a Pastor to this church. I'm sure you're aware he is now the President."

"Tell him I want him to meet me here in my home. In case he has forgotten, my address it's 35 Apple Lane, County Armagh, Ireland, Postcode: BT32 6NI."

"Sir, President Edwards will probably be too busy. You'll probably have to contact him directly to organise such an arrangement. I'd suggest trying to get in touch with him through the White House."

"Well, could you take my details in case you ever meet him?"

He agrees, and I end the call. I pause for a moment then put on my trench coat and go on my usual route around the countryside, pretending to be the Irish revolutionary Michael Collins. I speak in a Cork accent and recite quotes or lines from the Irish leader. Stephanie O'Reilly is my Kitty Kiernan, and Dad's farm is just like Collins' in Cork. I have a similar upbringing, plus the determination and ability to bring about significant political change as he did.

I walk around the farm and talk to myself about what I see.

It's nearly two weeks since I was diagnosed with akathisia. I come down the back lane from another one of my walks. Several cars are parked in the yard including a Porsche Macan, clearly the big-shot consultant's, which I can't take my eyes off. I make my way into the house. As I take off my wellingtons and coat in the utility room, Mum and Dad come and tell me to make my way into the living room. I walk in and take a seat, smiling at the two nurses and Dr Smith. Mum and Dad are also in the room. Dr Smith talks about readmitting me to the hospital.

No, no, no. This can't be happening. How am I going to get out of this one?

"Look, I'm absolutely fine."

"Your mum and dad disagree," Dr Smith says. "They say the akathisia is getting worse. They say you're even more restless, going for even more walks and finding it impossible to

MANIC

rest or sit still. They're worried that you'll relapse into another episode like you had before Christmas, and nobody wants that to happen."

"But there is nothing wrong with me." Okay, the akathisia is still an issue but that is merely a side effect. Other than that, I'm fine.

There is a pause then Dr Smith uncrosses her legs. "Currently there aren't any free beds in the hospital. Although your condition isn't desirable, we can monitor it until a bed becomes available. We've changed your medication, so hopefully, that'll make a difference."

Thank Mary, the mother of God. I sigh and I feel a smile on my face as there's no threat of readmission, at least not today. Hey, I might just toy with these health professionals a bit.

I smile and stifle a laugh. "You know, you're right, but really I think I need a psychologist, not a psychiatrist. I need hugs, not drugs. I'd like to request one. I'm not expecting Sigmund Freud, Carl Jung or Erik Erikson but a psychologist I can talk to; that will be more conducive to my recovery."

Dr Smith rubs her chin. She stutters or has difficulty in finding the right words. Then she merely tells me I'll be going to the hospital in the next few days. When she says this, I feel my grin disappear but I'm not giving up that easily.

"Well, could you take me to the hospital in your nice Porsche?"

Everyone in the room laughs in such a way that would make even Spiffy Jenkins go red with envy. Dr Smith goes red but I doubt it's because of envy. Once everyone regains their composure, she kindly declines my request.

But for real, I can't be readmitted to the hospital so I repeat my mantra: "There's nothing wrong with me."

21

MESSIAH

Friday 28th February

Early the next morning, I walk my usual route around the country roads, flicking out the blade of my Swiss Army knife and then closing it again. I use it around the farm to cut open bags and bales. As I approach the front lane, a thought comes to my mind. Am I the Messiah? I am a type of messiah. One capable of greatness. One who will go down in history. A century after my death, children will learn of my glorious deeds in school. I am Jesus Christ and Stephanie is my bride, the church, whom I need to save from the Satanic manipulation of Colin.

This lane is the narrow road that goes to the new Jerusalem. The passage of my triumphant entry as the King of kings and Lord of lords. But I have no steed to carry me along the way. No rapturous crowds are there to beckon me on. Will

MANIC

angels now descend from Heaven in all their glory, playing the harp, lyre and trumpet, praising me?

Then Spiffy Jenkins speaks to me. *Now, Niall. I'm an atheist but I love playing along with your ideas. So, of course, I get that you're the incarnation of a non-existent being, fabricated by a group of misogynistic men who were just as psychotic as you are. So, yeah, you are the Messiah. Let's pretend. Listen to all those people shouting your name, Niall. I mean, Jesus. Look at all those cloaks. I say invisible cloaks. Play along, Niall. You know what to do. Come on, this is your moment. Pretend you're riding upon a colt over the cloaks. You're on a colt going over a cloak. Say it, Niall. Come on, you're on a colt going over a cloak. Say it. Imagine if Stephanie was here, she'd be so impressed.*

I say it repeatedly and crawl on all fours. I'm a donkey, but every so often I stand up straight and spin around.

"Hosanna, Hosanna to Stephanie O'Reilly, my bride and church."

I keep repeating this as I walk along the lane. At the halfway point, I pass the miry ditch of water that's stagnant. I throw several stones into it.

"The abomination that causes desolation; the cesspool of sin and degradation."

Come on, Niall. It's a stream your dad foolishly polluted.

Jenkins' words put me into a rage.

"I curse it because it brings no life."

Well, I'm sure there are plenty of other streams that give life although I wouldn't recommend the Thames. You're probably best not knowing what's in it.

"I'm the water of life," I yell.

Oh, I forgot you are totally bonkers. There is no point in trying to reason with you, so I'm not going to bother.

The voice goes silent. I stand proud, for I have won the argument. I enter the house and go into the kitchen.

I sit at the table with a tin of beans and a packet of crisps. Then Colin speaks to me. Yes, that's right, Colin the idiot from the hospital is talking to me.

Turn the beans and crisps into a steak dinner.

"What?" I shout.

MARK BROWNLEE

If you are the Son of God, you can perform miracles. You can turn this measly food into something more appealing.

"I don't need to."

Because you can't.

"Don't put your Lord, your God, to the test."

Funny, the real Son of God said that once, only He was humbly referring to His heavenly Father, and not Himself.

"What do you want, Colin?"

Unite yourself to God by slitting your wrists. Surely you will go to Heaven if you are the Son of God.

"Madness. I will not do that. What are you going to say now, Colin, or should I call you by your proper name, Satan? Are you going to promise all powers and kingdoms if I bow down and worship you?"

Why would I do that?

"Because I am the Messiah, and I will marry Stephanie one day."

I think not. I've got her wrapped around my little finger. She thinks nothing of you. You're that crazy, that far gone, that you think Stephanie would be interested in a guy like you, who thinks he's the Messiah.

"Come on, Colin. Has the cat got your tongue?"

Niall, you're the one person in the whole universe God should have decreed to come out of his mother's ass rather than her front.

If Colin needs to go out of his way to discourage me and prevent me from believing I am the Messiah, it's proof I am the saviour of the world. It must mean I have a future with Stephanie. Yet, despite being the water of life, I'm incredibly thirsty. I go to the kitchen tap, fill a glass and down it in one gulp, spilling some water onto my face then rub my cheeks with the sleeve of my jumper.

There's a voice coming from the living room. James Edwards? My face lights up. I dash in in a frenzy but when I enter, nobody's there. The TV is playing the President's inaugural speech to Congress. He is calling for unity and asking the two main parties to unite and come together. To find a common purpose despite their differences. I had come to the attention of Edwards, my mentor. I had spoken to him on Dad's

MANIC

birthday. Soon we'll be united again. I'm mesmerised, hanging on his every word. Edwards is the incarnation of God the Father, while I am the incarnation of God the Son.

Dad's farm will now become a religious site, more sacred than Jerusalem and Mecca combined. Armagh will be the new Jerusalem and there will no longer be any other religions – all will worship me. Both cathedrals in Armagh will be bulldozed, and one single temple will be rebuilt, ten times the original size of the Catholic cathedral. Armagh will have a population of millions and will become a thriving Metropolis. It'll not just have church spires, but the tallest skyscrapers ever constructed as quite literally the entire world's population will flock to the city. In mere days, it'll surpass the economic and cosmopolitan hubs of New York and London. The sheer number of people all seeking to have a glimpse of the Son of God will establish Armagh as the centre of the universe. I will rule the world under one flag, king and religion. I'll bring world peace, end world hunger and poverty.

My new followers are coming to me. I scream at the top of my voice repeatedly, "Come to me; worship me." Nothing happens. Perhaps I should pray, using the rosary. I frantically fiddle with the beads, bowing my head, and mumble to God. Still, nothing happens. I throw the rosary beads across the floor. I'm beyond prayer; after all, I'm the Son of God. It's God's duty that He answers my demands and pleas.

I huff as I walk out of the kitchen to my room and stare at a mirror hanging on the wall. I have never been so mesmerised by my reflection. I smile as I stare at the face of God. I'm beautiful, angelic. More impressive than any angel. Then there's a voice.

Men look at the outward appearance. I see the heart, and your heart is a cesspool of filthy pride that's a stench to all who lay eyes on you.

"Colin?" I cry. "Is that you? What would you know about having a pure heart? When yours has always been full of evil and pride."

Look into the mirror, Niall. What do you see?

"Christ," I say.

No, the voice replies. *You see the Antichrist.*

MARK BROWNLEE

"No, that's not true. Lies, lies. I am the Christ," I scream.

I pick up a vase from the windowsill and smash it against the mirror. I fall onto the floor, red-faced and sobbing. Peering up, I see Conor is in the doorway.

"Niall! Why did you smash the mirror?"

I do not respond. He persists. Each time he asks me a question, I stare into space. He tries to catch my gaze, but still, I say nothing.

"Niall, look at me. Stay here while I call the home treatment team." I'm silent only for a moment, then I get up and follow him.

More subdued, I walk with him along the hallway. He glances back and sighs. He smiles at me and gestures for me to come with him to the kitchen So I follow him. There he stands with other family members who have just arrived back. They all stare at me. I'm dizzy.

"Niall? Niall, are you alright?" Conor asks as I fall to the floor and he tries to catch me.

I lie on the floor then jump up, smiling as my family watches me. I stare at each one of them.

"Worship me."

My family remains silent.

"Worship me, Stephanie," I repeat. Still, they remain silent. Why don't they get it? I'm the Messiah. Why don't they worship me? I turn my face up to the ceiling and scream at the top of my voice, "Father God, crown me, crown me."

I wait for some change of circumstance. My family are still all here, but neither Stephanie nor any of my new followers have entered the house to worship me.

Why is my family speechless? Their silence is because they're in awe of me. I grin at them with their wide eyes and open mouths. A verse from scripture comes to my mind: *the fear of the Lord is the beginning of wisdom* (Proverbs 9:10). Then I consider what the voice had told me earlier. Is my family misleading me? Are they devils worshipping the great Beelzebub? Adrenaline rushes through my body and I grit my teeth as I turn to Dad and attempt to strangle him. My hands clutch his neck as hard as I can. His face turns purple then blue as Conor and everyone else tries to restrain me.

MANIC

Soon, my family is grabbing me, trying to get me to release Dad. I let go before he passes out. I stare at the other demons that possess my family. I go for Dad and throw a fist at him. He falls to the ground. I go for him again but Conor grasps me before the blow meets its mark.

Dad regains his composure while Conor distracts me. Dad winds me with a fist to the chest and I fall to the floor in pain.

"Leave him," Mum screams and Dad has the sense to stop. After all, he's sober.

I stand up but wobble. Before I can straighten up, I fall to the floor again and pass out.

I open my eyes to two male police officers staring at me. Dad is cross-faced with arms folded. I stare at the two police officers. "Am I in trouble, officers?"

Both turn to Dad, who pauses for a while. "Cuff him, let's be on the safe side." Both officers are big and taller than me, making it impossible for me to resist. They pick me up And I struggle, to no avail. My limbs shake and my beating heart causes a pain in my chest.

"No, no, you can't do this! I'm sorry. I didn't mean to hurt anybody. Please, you have to believe me."

I guess it's too late for all that.

They restrain me, despite my pleas. I scan around the room at my family. What have I done?

"I'm sorry," I say, as the police officers take me away.

22

GETHSEMANE

Friday 28th February

pace along the corridor in the hospital, grasping my Swiss Army knife in my pocket.

"Doctor Henson would like to speak to you now," Christine says.

I make my way to the interview room and peer into the window at Henson, who is studiously writing notes. I go in and he glances up from his work.

"It seems you've had quite an eventful day. Can you tell me about it in your own words?" he says, flicking through the pages of my file.

I tell him everything that happened to which he says, "Is

MANIC

there anything else you would like to say?"

I sigh. "I need your help."

Dr Henson nods, straight-faced.

"I want you to write my story after I die."

"Why would I do that?"

"You know me. Look at the huge file with my name on it. You can write my story with it."

He closes the folder and holds it in front of me. "This is confidential information. I'd lose my job if I did such a thing."

I break down and cry. It's all too much. "I'm about to die. I need somebody to write my story to stop me from being forgotten as a nobody. Edwards wants me to be Niall Alexander the Great. But I …"

He leans back in his chair and folds his arms.

I continue. "I'm the Messiah and James Edwards told me I have a mission to conquer Russia. But I just can't do it." I cry as my face falls into my hands.

He places a hand on my shoulder. "Niall, you said you talked to Edwards. When was this?"

I raise my head and wipe the tears from my face. "After I was discharged."

Henson gazes up at something on the ceiling. "Where were you when you talked to him?"

"In my home."

"And was there anybody else with you in the room?" he enquires.

"No."

"Niall, do you know what a hallucination is?"

I do. Yet I know who I talked to was as real as you are in front of me now. I continue to sob and beg on my hands and knees in front of him. "Doctor. Please help me. I …"

He stares at me for a long time before speaking again. "We're done here, Niall. By the sounds of things, we might have to keep you here for a while," he says, closing my file on his lap.

We both leave as I go to the canteen and slowly regain my composure. Martin walks along the corridor to the canteen. He doesn't seem to notice me as I walk behind him. I sit with him at one of the tables with Ramona and Christopher.

MARK BROWNLEE

"Hi. How have things been for you?" I ask Martin weakly.

"Fine."

But the red marks around his neck tell a very different story. The same marks I had when I tried to hang myself. Clearly, that's what he wanted to talk to me about when I tried to complete suicide in the hospital. He was thinking of doing it himself and wanted tips.

There's a silence between us for a time. Then I ask if he's interested in playing a game of chess. He nods and goes into the interview room while I get the board. We sit at the table and assemble the pieces silently. It's a close-fought game but I win in the end, not that the outcome really matters to either one of us.

After the game, Martin continues to rub the marks on his neck. "You tried killing yourself, Niall."

I hesitate, looking back on the time I slit my wrists. The time of darkness when I thought death was the only form of relief. But I don't want to entertain that thought. It's only a freight train to Hell.

"Look, Martin, it seems we've both been in dark places. It's best if we don't dwell on them too much."

"I've been thinking about it a lot. That eerie feeling of darkness seems to fall over me like a misty fog. There is no light and I don't know if the fog will lift," he says, face downcast.

"Hopefully, things will get better," I say weakly.

"I hope you're right."

I try to speak with some conviction, but Martin doesn't appear to respond to my message that time will change things for the better. I try to hold a blank face as he stares out of the window. I say nothing for a minute. I sit with him uncomfortably before he responds.

"Maybe you're right. I need a good night's sleep. That might help."

"How has your sleep been lately?" I ask.

"Not great."

"Chat to one of the nurses; they might be able to give you a sleeping tablet."

I'm struggling with whether I can go on myself. Thoughts of ending it all descend on me not like a cloud but a mist that I

MANIC

wish would just envelope me into a state of non-existence. I know I'm Catholic but forget about the afterlife. I don't want any form of life right now, I just want nothing. The way things were before I was born. Oh, how I wish I was never born right now.

When evening comes and we are all getting our medication, Martin and I are near the front. Colin arrives late and stands a few people back. All the patients are standing in a line curving along the hallway. The nurses are five minutes late but quickly set out the plastic cups and medication containers on the metal trolley for each patient.

Ramona comes along the corridor with her long greasy hair, her head extended forward slightly, like a strutting hen. She's wearing a long black dress with holes in it and heavy-duty boots. When she reaches the medication room with the other patients, she bellows curses and insults at the nurses for not being faster in administering the drugs. Then her speech becomes completely incoherent.

Most of the patients ignore her but I can't. Are her incoherent utterances prophetic and do they refer to me? She reminds me of myself when I was psychotic, when I thought the wrath of Edwards and the Russians would rest on me and that it would result in a nuclear holocaust. Once again, paranoia rises in my brain. When I receive my medication, I immediately go to my room and write a poem on five points of human history. Each stanza is a stage of human existence, the last being the most terrifying.

"We lived like we had no meaning
no ultimate reason to exist
death became the only meaningful thing
ending what had become meaningless."

I tremble as I read the last stanza. The thought of suicide continues to linger in my head. Could I do it again? Then the idea of Hell suddenly terrifies me. Am I righteous enough to get into Heaven or even Purgatory? Am I destined to spend an eternity in Hell for my sins? There will be no opportunity for me to be the victorious general parading around Europe. I'd be incinerated like most of the rest of humanity as the result of

MARK BROWNLEE

nuclear war, and with the condemnation of God upon us, which will lead to eternal torment.

I go over to my artbook, turn to a blank page, and write at the top of it, 'the age of consolation'. I write the number one at the bottom and draw the rough outline of a cross. Then, turning over to the next page, I write at the top, 'the age of rejection', create a large X in the middle and then write the number two at the bottom of the page. On page number three, the title is, 'the age of hedonism' and a dollar sign is drawn. The next page is 'the age of scepticism' and a question mark is created. Lastly, page number five represents 'the age of extinction' and a man in flames is drawn.

Then in a complete frenzy, I rip the pages from the spine of the book. Grabbing them, I tear them into several pieces and throw them up in the air, like a judgemental creator destroying his creation. I let out a sigh as the scraps descend onto the floor. One page mainly survives my wrath. The side that faces up to me is blank. I pick it up and take it to the table. I had drawn a bird's-eye view of the mall of Armagh on the page. It's coffin shape represents the outlining path around the grass area and two paths that run across its middle. One of these has the cenotaph to the Boer Wars in the middle of it. My drawing of the memorial fixates me. I stare at it for a while with a stern face.

"That's where the British were the Nazis." Then, holding the paper over the edge of the table, I stab it with my pen, creating a hole and a tear across it where I have drawn the cenotaph. I sit quietly for a time and I think of all the points in history where the British oppressed the Irish. The atrocity at Drogheda in the 17th century by Oliver Cromwell when his troops cried, "To Hell or Connaught" as they breached the walls. I face a similar choice since I believe my hope of Heaven is gone, and I only have two options to continue to live (Connaught) or experience eternal damnation (Hell). I write three words spread across the top of the page, 'Hell or Connaught'. I consider each option carefully and, in the end, choose life, at least for now. I lift the page to the light above my head and pierce a hole with my pen above the word 'Connaught'. But as I do so, the light shines through the page,

MANIC

revealing my previous creation of the man in a fire that represents man's final state, 'the age of extinction'. I stare at this image of the man in flames and look at all my other drawings of human existence ripped up on the floor. I haven't a choice between Hell or Connaught, life or death. Hell is my only choice. I raise the page, pierce a hole above the word Hell and throw the sheet onto the ground in dismay. After bowing my head for a short while, I glare at the discarded page lying on the floor. I consider the three holes pierced through the paper. Two at the top, one at the bottom with a tear across it. It's the face of Beelzebub himself, staring up at me from the depths of Hell, grinning at me and speaking to me: *The end is near, Niall. Soon you will meet your end.* Death spreads inside my mind like a fire. Sweat bleeds from my face as I whisper to God, "Take this cup away from me." But it's all in vain. I take out my pocketknife, roll up my sleeve and place the knife on the same wrist of my previous attempt. I notice all the pink scars. I close my eyes and grit my teeth then I hear my phone ping.

It's Stephanie on Messenger.

-Hey, Niall. Sorry for not keeping in touch. Colin can be a jerk sometimes and it has rubbed off on me. I'm in Paris with my mum. If you give me your address, I can send you a postcard.

She's in Paris. Her first time out of the North and I'm not there with her.

-Sure, I would love that. My address is:
35 Apple Lane,
County Armagh,
BT32 6NI."
-Cheers. I look forward to seeing you in hospital.
-Yeah, I'd like that.

I put the knife back into my pocket and cover my wrist with my sleeve.

23

THE STRANGER

Saturday 29th February

The next day, two student doctors, one male, one female, are currently being shown around the ward by Doctor Henson. They stand outside the staff base as I pace back and forth from the canteen to my room. The akathisia is still a real pain. When I pass them, Doctor Henson opens the staff-base door.

"Niall, are you free? I was wondering if you would answer a few questions from these doctors?"

"Sure."

The three of us make our way to the interview room. I sit on one side while they sit on the other with curious looks on

MANIC

their faces. They introduce themselves as Liam and Sharon.

"So, how is it that you found yourself in the hospital?" Liam asks in a thick Scottish accent.

"I had an episode before Christmas."

"Can you describe your experiences relating to that episode?"

"How do you mean?" I ask.

"Well, when it comes to psychotic episodes, there are three common experiences: delusions, illusions and hallucinations. A delusion is an irrational belief that contradicts reality. An illusion is a distorted perception of reality, while a hallucination is a distorted perception that has no reality at all. Are you experiencing any of these at present?"

To be honest, I've no idea of the differences this guy has just described. I'm not really sure if I'm experiencing any at the minute. Hang on, maybe that's not totally true. I smile, realising these are med students. I'll be a bit pretentious and try to impress with my knowledge of mental health.

"I would describe my current mental state as psychologically sane, sociologically insane."

They turn to each other before Liam responds, "Doesn't that make you a robot?"

"That's one way of looking at me for you 'hippo-crates'."

The two of them glance at each other, probably thinking I had called them hypocrites. Realising this, I clarify through more careful pronunciation of the word 'hip-poc-rates' before they understand what I'm trying to say.

They both nod. "Yes, we both hold to ethical standards not to harm our patients, Niall."

Liam rests his face on his hand. "Niall, I was wondering whether you could tell us if you've ever had a hallucination?"

I wonder if Henson has already given them the low down. He raised that red herring with me yesterday.

I sigh. "That's a difficult question to answer. I can only know for sure if somebody else can confirm they can't see what I see."

Liam rubs his chin. "Or something appeared abnormal, in retrospect."

Like when I saw the familiars on people's shoulders during

172

my episode in the hospital. Then when I saw James Edwards in my house on my dad's birthday. Was that real? Is anything real? No, I trust my senses in my current state. To Hell with everyone else. Reality will now be determined solely by my senses, no matter what anybody says. My reality is the only true reality. But where will this lead me?

I look directly at Liam. "Unfortunately, I find it hard to put it into words."

He drops his hand from his chin. I smile at each of them before he responds. "We have no further questions."

With that, he stands up and offers his hand to me, which I shake. Sharon gives me a hesitant smile and nod. We leave the room and the two of them go back to the staff base. They're talking to Doctor Henson. Then Jim walks over from the canteen. I'm bored and tap the floor ceaselessly with my foot.

"Would you be interested in taking part in a table quiz up in the canteen?" he asks.

"Sure."

I enter the canteen and take a seat at a table with Colin and Martin. Colin frowns at me. What's his problem?

I smile as I sit down beside him. Quizzes are my forte. I sit, shaking my left leg in the same repetitive motion, my toes raised and my knees going up and down like the rod of a locomotive, while the rest of my body remains static.

"Are you having a fit or something? Can't you sit still for a minute?" Colin asks.

"I've akathisia," I respond.

"What's that?"

"It's a condition that gives restless legs."

"Well, if you can't sit still, you'd be better off doing something else rather than taking part in this quiz."

I immediately stop shaking my legs and try to stay as motionless as possible. While I do so, Jim begins the next round of the quiz.

"The next round is on literature. Question one. Which author once said, 'The demand that I make of my reader is that he should devote his whole life to reading my works'?"

Patients confer with one another quietly. I can't help but blurt out, "That's easy." Yet as I do so, Colin writes the answer

M A N I C

'William Shakespeare'. Shakespeare?

"No, that's not right. It's James Joyce," I say.

"Niall, don't shout out," Martin says.

"It's not," Colin responds as he shakes his head.

"How would you know? You're a jock."

He stands up and glares at me then sits down.

"Okay," I say sarcastically. "I was only trying to help."

He stands up again. This time, he swings at me.

"Leave him alone, Colin. He isn't well," Martin says calmly, a hand on Colin's shoulder.

I turn to Jim, my arms folded. "James Joyce. I'm positive."

"You don't need to raise your voice," Martin says.

"I'm right."

"No, you're not," Colin retorts.

"How would you know?"

"Niall, there's no need to make a scene. It's just a quiz," Martin says, gesturing to me to sit down.

Colin grins. "Oh, and by the way, Niall, I know you were talking to my girl last night on Messenger. If you ever talk to her again, I'll suffocate you in your sleep."

I have a sudden sensation of increased strength and an edgy, twitchy feeling. I mean, who does he think he is? Something is taking over me. It's not just anger, but I don't know what it is. I need to leave before I do something I will later regret. I can no longer reflect on things, only react to the situations of my reality. Something is brooding inside me.

I bolt up off my chair and leave the canteen with a heavy posture to my walk as I stride along the hallway to the staff base. I have my hands in my pocket and kick my right leg across my left. Christine asks how I'm doing. I stop and turn to her. I'm sweating and my hands are clammy. My heartbeat lowers as I take a deep breath and slowly pace towards her in the doorway.

"I'm fine," I say, but of course, I've been better.

"Well, do you mind if I take your blood pressure?" Actually, I kind of do. I don't want her to find out I'm not okay. But then, if I refuse, she'll assume that anyway.

I nod. "Yeah, that's fine."

I take several deep breaths and sit outside the staff base.

174

Christine wheels a blood pressure monitor to the left of me. I unzip my jumper and raise my left arm into a horizontal position as she places the strap around my bicep. I continue to breathe loudly in and out as it tightens around my arm. It squeezes my bicep to such an extent that it's painful. She monitors the results that are displayed on the machine. The digits on the monitor run up and down. As time goes on, they lose pace and they settle at a number. I'm unsure what the reading means.

"Am I okay?"

Christine laughs. "Yes, your blood pressure is completely normal."

I smile at a new patient standing outside the staff base, waiting for someone to come to him. He's a tall, slim boy around sixteen with a skinhead. He wears a black t-shirt revealing cuts inside his arms. The t-shirt also has cigarette ash on the front of it. He wears muddy combat trousers, meant to be grey, and a pair of heavy-duty boots, the leather cut off the right steel toe cap. His face is red and his eyes have an edgy look to them. When the other nurse in the staff base comes out to talk to him, I try to listen in to their conversation but they're too far away. When the conversation ends, he moves over and stands in front of me. He's on the phone to somebody. I listen in as the conversation comes to an end.

"I'm so sorry to hear she died. Goodbye," he says, then hangs up.

I frown. Who's dead? Stephanie? Wait, no? Yes, it makes perfect sense. You can tell he's a rough kid with mental issues that some gang paid to kill Stephanie. My eyes widen. My muscles tense up. I'm sitting near Stephanie's murderer? I'm trying really hard not to crap myself. What about my family? Are they safe? Or are they going to be killed too? Although I'm in luck. He's small, nowhere near as intimidating as Colin.

I grab him by his collar. "You killed Stephanie?" I cry as I try to hold back the tears that flood from my eyes.

"I don't know who Stephanie is," the boy says, shaking.

I shout, "Tell me the truth. Where is she? Where did you bury her?"

"I don't know what you're talking about."

MANIC

I throw him to the ground, realising he is merely a pawn. But if he is merely a pawn, who are the major chess pieces? This goes right to the top, ever since Edwards told me his plan to conquer Russia. This kid's been paid by the Russian mafia to take me out. Or maybe it's the Russian Government. Yeah, like there's a difference?

I run to my room, wiping the tears from my face. Thrusting the door open, I leap over the bed, kicking clothes onto the ground. I grab the *Wrath* poem, the one I wrote in the art room, and rush to the staff base to find Doctor Henson. He has his back turned to me as he sits at a computer monitor. I stand impatiently outside before erratically knocking on the window in the door. I hit ceaselessly until the door opens.

"Calm down, Niall. There's nothing wrong."

"Don't tell me to calm down because everything is wrong. Take this poem."

"Why?"

"I want you to take it and make copies and send them to *The Irish News, The Irish Times* and *The Times* newspapers because they're going to be published in tomorrow's editions."

The doctor asks me, "And why would they do that?"

"Because I'm about to be assassinated by the Spetsnaz. They've already murdered my Stephanie, and now they're coming for me. This poem describes Edwards' wrath that needs to be poured out against the Russians." I say all this because I'm convinced I'm a walking dead man.

"She's dead," I yell, throwing the poem at him as my body chills and I have a stabbing stomach pain. There's a growing tightness in my chest that will not loosen. An infusion of adrenaline rocks my body as I stride along the corridor to the canteen. I enter and scream at the top of my voice.

"I'm about to be assassinated, and none of you seem to give a toss. You're just playing your stupid quiz."

No one responds. Jim stops reading out the answers from the previous round. Christine paces along the corridor and takes me by the hand along to the staff base. She gestures to me to stand outside while she waits to speak to Doctor Henson. He's on the phone, talking to the newspapers about my drawings. Once he puts the phone down, he briefly chats to

MARK BROWNLEE

Christine, and as she opens the door, he says I've got a visitor.

"Okay, I'll bring her in," Christine replies.

"Who is my visitor?" Neither Christine nor Henson respond to my question.

"Niall, it's best if you spend some time in your room."

"I'm about to die."

Christine takes me by the arm and my emotions become less heightened. She even manages to get me to lie down on my bed for several moments. While my head rests on my hands and bent arms, my mind races on. Who is my visitor? Could it be her? Her? Is she dead or alive? What is her name? It's the trauma that's messing with my head. My lover, the girl who is currently going out with Colin. I can't remember her name. I now refer to her as the stranger. Is she still alive? Or is she now a phantom or a ghost? Maybe she found out how bad I was and cut her trip short. I try to go on my phone but for some reason it's dead. My time is short before my inevitable death. My mind hurtles through a jumble of disconnected images, spiking as my agitation grows. I feel fatigue from all the tension in my body. The Spetsnaz are coming to kill me? Maybe the stranger is still alive. Martin is working for the Russian government and is holding the stranger hostage. Will he kill her out of jealousy?

I jolt up on my bed, jump towards the door and clumsily open it, almost falling over. I sprint along the hallway. I hope to unravel the possibility of Martin having any evil intent on his mind. Both feet slide forward as I stop abruptly in front of the window of the staff base. There's a woman wearing a nurse's uniform who resembles the stranger. She has the same ginger hair but is shorter and has more freckles on her face. She's not exactly like her, but is it the stranger, using supernatural powers to take the form of someone else so that she can be with me in the hospital? I go to find Martin in the canteen area but the quiz has already finished. The place is empty. I go back to the staff base. Is the new nurse still there? She's gone. Martin has taken her into her room and tied her up. I push open his bedroom door. He's at his desk.

"Where is the stranger?" I shout.

"I don't know what you're talking about," he says, with scrunched eyebrows and his head tilted to the side.

MANIC

"Yes, you do. You've taken my girlfriend from me and you were going to kill her."

"Niall, you're freaking me out. I don't know where your girlfriend is."

"Yes, you do. You're hiding her. She is in the shower room."

I slowly open the shower-room door, trembling – what will I find? Perhaps the dead body of the stranger. Or maybe a view of her struggling about on the floor, hands and feet tied and a gag in her mouth. When I open the door, there's nothing but an empty shower room. The only things present are a selection of toiletries on the sink.

The revelation is testimony to Martin's innocence. Where is the stranger? She is in the ward somewhere. I search everywhere. I even go into other people's rooms but I can't find her. Then, when I pass the interview room, there's a woman roughly the same age as the stranger and who has all the same physical attributes except that she has blonde hair and is slightly overweight. My eyes are on the woman who smiles and gives me a wave. I freeze. The stranger is definitely a shapeshifter, someone who is able to take the shape or form of any human being. Before I avail myself of the opportunity of chatting to this new visitor, Christine grabs me by the hand and takes me back to my room.

"Niall, your behaviour is annoying a lot of the other patients, especially going into their rooms. If you could please stay in your room. How about you draw something or write a poem? Jim says you are really good at that."

I sit at my desk, wondering for the next few moments where the stranger might be.

24

CALVARY

Saturday 29th February –

Sunday 1st March

The wind blows through the curtains into the room. A door outside bangs. What's that? Gunfire? My shoulder is against my bedroom door. Got to stop the Spetsnaz from coming in. They're here! The voices: *Crucify him! Crucify him!* I am the Lord's Messiah and they'll rejoice in my pain and suffering. I am Jesus, God, Your son. Help me, Lord God! Please help me.

I fall onto the floor and shake incessantly. I scream at another loud bang and a yell. I scream again in my darkened room until, moments later, the door opens and someone stands over me. I shuffle into the corner of the room, weeping

MANIC

like a baby.

"Please don't hurt ... please don't hurt me."

"Niall, no one is going to harm you." Their voice is familiar. It's Christine.

"Yes, they are. They're trying to kill me and everybody else in this hospital."

"No one is trying to kill you."

"Christine, they're going to kill you as well. I can't let that happen. It's me they want."

I can save everybody by trying to reason with the Spetsnaz outside. I get up from the floor and pass Christine in the doorway. I stand in front of a fire exit that I can't open. I stare out into the night. Is anybody there? Nobody, yet something terrible is about to happen. So, I imitate the shape of the cross with legs together and my arms out straight. I hope I will signal to those outside that I'm willing to die alone while everyone else on the ward will be allowed to live. Yet, as I give my sign of the cross, no signal comes back to me from the outside.

I turn around and dash along to the other end of the corridor, to the other fire exit. Again, I imitate the shape of the cross with my body but there's nothing outside. I keep running to each fire exit, repeating the signal countless times. The lack of response must mean my signalling is working, delaying the Spetsnaz from taking any action, at least for now.

I pray. "Mother Mary, I don't know what to do right now. I've had a terrifying day. I can't stop this hospital from going up in flames, and I've no idea where the stranger is. I can't even remember her name."

A voice speaks to me, *Look up to your right*. I look up at the door of my en suite bathroom, which is closed. I freeze for a moment and then I shake. Is the stranger hiding in the shower room? Hiding? Seeking refuge from the carnage that's about to begin? I'm horrified by the picture of the stranger lying on the bathroom floor. I break down and cry at the image in my head.

"Stranger, are you in there?"

Silence.

"I love you. You are the one person I care about the most,

MARK BROWNLEE

and it breaks my heart that harm would come to you."

No reply is made. I can't bring myself to open it, to a scene that will haunt me for the rest of my life. I wipe the tears with the sleeve of my jumper. At least I now know where my lover is. It's a matter of somehow getting her out of the hospital before the place is destroyed. My only hope is that Edwards will do something to save us.

There is an emergency telephone outside my room. I try to use it to communicate with Edwards. How will he save us? He'll intervene by sending a rapid response team to extract us. A Chinook helicopter will descend to take us away from the hospital. I press the buttons of the telephone and speak into the receiver.

"Tell Edwards to send the Chinook before midnight," I say.

With that, I shoot back into my room and wait.

Midnight passes with no attack and no Chinook comes to take us away. I still need to escape this place. Hang on, yes, I could do it like the magnificent Mr Toad in *The Wind in the Willows*. He did it by befriending the washer lady who aided him in his escape from prison. That's it. All I have to do is befriend one of the nurses, and they will let me walk out of the hospital scot-free. They will unlock one of the fire exit doors and there, waiting for me, will be US military personnel ready to take me away.

Grinning, I walk to the staff base where the night staff are present. I stand in the doorway and address them.

"Can the magnificent Mr Toad convince this beautiful young lady and the handsome young gentleman to allow him to go home to Toad Manor?"

They smile and laugh. "How about the magnificent Mr Toad go and wait quietly in his room, and we'll see what we can do."

"Really?" I say, breaking out of character.

"Yes."

"Cool. I'll pack my bags."

"You do that as long as you stay in your room."

I walk briskly along the corridor to my room. I place my backpack on the bed and put my clothes into it. When the bag is almost full, I put in my Bible and crucifix then I throw the bag

MANIC

on my back and step out of my room. I stand patiently in front of the fire exit where I expect, at any moment, the doors will be unlocked by the nurses, and a US Chinook helicopter will take us away to safety.

I stand, but nothing happens. I wait and watch outside where the sun is rising. I look out for any military personnel or hardware. I pick up the emergency phone to contact Mr Edwards directly. I press the buttons as I did before. The line is completely dead. I push all the buttons out of frustration. In doing so, I inadvertently press a button that lights up the screen on the handset, making the words 'enter keycode' run across the screen. Keycode? Of course, all I have to do now is enter the correct keycode and the fire exit will open. I type in the four digits of my birthday. I try to pull open the door. It's still locked. I let out a sigh, bowing my head in dismay.

I press another four-digit number. I push and pull the fire exit door aggressively – it won't budge. I keep repeating this process all morning without either of the two nurses on shift able to stop me. Once the morning staff come in, I stop and go back to my room.

There's a release of tension in my body when there's no attack and I'm still alive. I question my belief about the Spetsnaz trying to kill me, and I muster the courage to open my bathroom door where I don't find the body of the stranger. I'm now convinced that I must get out of the hospital immediately if I want to be with the stranger. Realising that I've so far failed, I have to rethink my strategy. I will have to get the support of other members of staff.

Liam is strolling along the corridor. I shout his name. He turns to me, and I hand him the piece of paper with the words *Get me out of here!* written on it. He opens it and reads it. I nod as my eyes are locked on his. He says nothing, yet I can now rely on him to help me escape. Now it's a matter of waiting for the opportune moment. The nurses are busier than usual this morning, leaving the staff base empty at times. Also, they have left the doors open. My eyes are glued to the staff base where Liam sits at a computer on his own. He's planning a way for me to escape. Then all of a sudden, he leaves the room vacant and walks to the canteen.

182

MARK BROWNLEE

I run into the staff base, take a seat on the computer chair and swing around on it. One of the camera views on the computer screens shows Liam heading towards the main exit. I rush out of the room to where he is. He is placing his key card to the sensor of the exit. I creep up behind him with such stealth that I sneak out with him as he opens the door. In the outside corridor he runs away from me. Why? He was the one that helped me escape.

I shout to him as I run. "Don't worry, the Magnificent Mister Toad has done this before."

His eyes widen and it dawns on me – he never meant to let me free. I turn back to Doctor Henson, along with three other nurses, now chasing me along the corridor. I sprint as fast as I can and outrun Henson and most of the nurses. However, a male nurse is gaining on me, and tackles me to the ground. I try to break free as the rest restrain me. There are too many of them, and they bring me back into the ward.

I turn to Henson and scream at the top of my voice, "Hannibal, I want to go home to Rome."

Colin and Martin – as well as the other patients – come out of their rooms to see the commotion. Martin removes his headphones and shakes his head while Colin squints, showing his teeth. With Christine, Jim leads all the patients away from viewing me. Other nurses come near me. Two of them stand at the ward's main entrance while another two go to either side of me. One tries to take me by the arm but I resist. "Don't touch me!" They want to move me somewhere else – where? Into some padded cell with a straightjacket on me where I'd be periodically electrocuted? I certainly can't let that happen without a fight. The more I fight, the more nurses come. I calm down when my mum comes in dressed as a nurse.

"Mumma? What are you doing here?"

She doesn't say anything.

"Please, Mum, they're going to put me into prison. Stop them."

She takes me by the arm and gets me to walk along the hallway to the lobby area with another nurse. The three of us eventually stand in front of double doors that are usually off-limits to patients on the ward. Now one of them opens the

MANIC

doors and directs me to go through them. I'm now going somewhere unfamiliar. My heart races and my limbs shake.

"You're going to put me in jail. You're going to put me into a tomb. I want to go home to Rome. Venus, I want to go home to Rome. Let me go home to Rome," I shout, then with head bowed I sob, "Where are you, Venus? Why, why have you forsaken me."

Tears stream down my face. As the nurses manage to get me to walk along the corridor, I slowly regain my composure but still let out a few sobs. We continue to walk further along the corridor. The walk seems to go on forever until we come to a door that requires one of the nurses to unlock it and we enter another ward. I shake because I will be staying here for the foreseeable future. I turn to the other nurse. It's her. It's her, my lover. I sob at her. "I'm sorry I've forgotten your name, stranger. Save me. Please save me, Venus."

Calmly, I think of how I'll escape as the nurses lead me along the end of the corridor to a set of double doors. One places a key card on the sensor and the door opens. "Are you going to lock me up?" I ask, yet no one responds. They lead me along another corridor to an entrance on the right, which has a sign saying 'Seclusion room' on it.

I enter this room. My Armagh GAA top is now soaked from all the sweat. The door shuts and automatically locks behind me.

I'm trapped.

I bang on the door with my fist, to no avail. My new accommodation is a small en suite room with a smell of alcohol and bleach. It's utterly empty except for some sheets, a mattress and a pillow in a corner. The friction tiles on the floor give an inhuman feel to the room. It's like animals are kept here. While the overall beige colour is nothing to be desired, the orange lighting perplexes me.

As I step into the en suite toilet, I close my eyes and imagine the stranger undressing in front of me. I only do so for a few moments before being overcome with shame. I press the sensor of the shower which sputters water down from above. The deluge comes down and I try to recite a poem I wrote about her.

After, I leap up and run to the window and bang on it with the palm of my hand.

"Get me the stranger. I need her. Get the stranger. She's all I want."

25

THE RETURN

Thursday 2ⁿᵈ April

wake up on the morning of Thursday the second of April and yawn. I'm now back on the normal ward with everybody else. I sit up on my bed, stretch and crack my knuckles. Rubbing the sleep from my eyes, I step into the en suite where I stare at my reflection in the mirror after shaving. I turn to my side and slide my right hand down my stomach. I turn ever so slightly left then right. Have I lost weight? I undress and get a shower. There is no doubt I am much better than what I was. But how long will they keep me before they think I am well enough to go home?

I bring my wooden chair over to my window. My feet are cold touching the metal bars in the sill. I sigh. Will I ever go out with Stephanie? I pull my hoody over my head and bow my face then look outside. Spring is making itself known as the

MARK BROWNLEE

grass is growing again. This morning, it's covered in a heavy dew and the trees are now re-clothed with new leaves. Each stands like a person as their branches blow in the harsh wind, like limbs, and bear down in the heavy rain. They remain constant and resolute to the elements, having the hope that the season is now turning in their favour. Birds sing, but despite considerable effort, I can't see them. Yet I believe in plenty of things that I can't see. Like the day I'll leave this place for good. Sure, I can see in the future but when will I see it in the present? I don't know – until that time, I live in hope.

There's a knock on the door, and a voice says, "Breakfast is ready." I'm not hungry yet but if I don't have something, I'll later regret it. Making my way to the canteen, I meet all the other patients, lining up behind them in the queue as the shutter rises. I receive my bowl of porridge and sit with Christopher, hoping nobody will speak to me. Once I sit down, I sing the song *Stephanie Says*. After all, I know she's the one.

Then Ramona turns to me. "Hey, do you like The Velvet Underground?"

"Yes, of course. Lou Reed was the prophet, priest and king of rock n roll."

"Awesome."

I'm actually astounded that somebody my age has actually heard of a small indie band from the sixties.

"What's your favourite song of theirs?"

"*I'm Sticking with You*. What about you?"

"*I'm Waiting for the Man*."

I laugh. "That song's about meeting a dealer in the street. Ramona, why am I not surprised?"

She cackles. "Whether it's hash, smack or snow, my dealer always knows how to put a smile on my face."

I subtly check her out. She's wearing a red tartan dress, hiking boots, white makeup, black lipstick and has long dark hair. Okay, not what I would usually go for but it's not like I have had a lot of choice ever since Stephanie left. I cross my legs and take another spoonful of cereal.

"I notice you always wear an Armagh top?"

"What can I say? I'm into football."

"Who's your local club?" she asks, spooning cereal into

MANIC

her mouth.

She's asking me about football but she's a goth.

"Collegeland. What about you?"

She pauses, gesturing that her mouth is full then replies after swallowing, "Crossmaglen Rangers."

Ramona likes The Velvet Underground and football. Did I miss something? Should I? No, Niall. Stephanie is the one, that will become clear. Forget about Ramona.

I nod. "That's not a bad club. They'll probably win the Armagh seniors. They have a good chance of winning the Ulster seniors as well; they've got a good team. Did you ever play any football yourself?"

She shakes her head. "Nah, being a girl, it was always camogie at our school."

She's not the one. Stick with Stephanie.

"I'd say those drugs probably wouldn't have helped you play," I joke.

"What? Of course, they would. They're great. You should try them."

"I'll pass on that."

I smile at her. I think I might have misjudged Ramona.

I finish my porridge and go on my usual circle around the ward since the akathisia is still affecting me. But today is different. I turn around the corner into the TV area where there is a large group of medical students with Doctor Henson peering down the other corridor. I stop and go back along the hallway.

Are all these students for me? I hate the fact that I've been walking all this time since coming out of the seclusion room and now I'm being stared at, like a lab rat, so I go back to my room. I throw myself onto the mattress and my eyes stare at the ceiling. I soon find myself restless again. Why can I not sit down or even lie down for any length of time? Why do I have to keep walking around and around like a robot? I lie there in despair until there's a gentle knock on the door. Christine enters the room.

"Niall, we would like you to have a meeting with Doctor Henson and the senior nurses of the ward."

I sit up. What could this be about? I stand and then slowly

MARK BROWNLEE

walk with him out into the corridor where I pass Christopher, who says nothing. I pass a nurse who is seated, observing Ramona in her room, before I go into the empty canteen. Finally, I stand before the doors of an interview room which is usually off-limits to patients on the ward.

We enter and Christine takes a seat with Jim, Doctor Henson and other nurses on one side of the table while I sit opposite on my own. Henson smiles at me before opening my medical file, which has significantly expanded since I was admitted to the hospital.

"Niall, you're here so we can review your progress and discuss a possible discharge from the hospital within the next few weeks."

I close my eyes, sigh and lean back into my chair. Discharge? Finally.

"So, how have you been?" he asks.

I nod. "Not too bad. The akathisia is still a nuisance."

"I noticed you this morning. You didn't walk around when the students were here."

He sure doesn't miss much in this lair of his. Fingers crossed I'll be leaving it sooner rather than later.

"I didn't want them to see me the way I was. It sucks to always be walking around in circles thinking you're a lunatic."

Yeah, I'm not being very PC with my terminology here but the akathisia has made me feel proper crazy.

"When we were here you didn't do that."

Fair point. "I know. I went and lay on my bed."

"That's progress. In regard to the akathisia, you might not necessarily be suffering from it; rather, it's more of a mental phenomenon. Your body's stuck in the same routine. With time, you'll slowly come out of it."

Yes, 'come out of it' sounds like great news, although I'm not sure about coming out of it 'slowly'.

"Why can't I come out of it now?"

"You'll need to be patient. We're all here today because we want to get your discharge right this time. None of us want you to be readmitted like you were the last time."

"When will I be discharged?"

"We don't want to set exact dates but within the next few

MANIC

weeks. Would that suit? Or is it too sudden?"

Oh, believe me, I wish discharge was as sudden as like right now but I know the akathisia is still an issue.

"No, that's fine." I need to be careful not to get my hopes up and besides, it's not like he said I was leaving today or tomorrow.

"We'd also like to talk a little bit about your plans when you leave the hospital for good." Doctor Henson glances up from the notes while fiddling with a pen and smiles. "People with your condition get all kinds of ideas of grandeur."

"Yes, for this upcoming year I'm going to take things easy but hopefully next year get my A-Levels and go to university the following year."

Then all my memories of being on the outside and going to school start to flood back. Maybe I'll have more of those philosophical conversations I had with my mate Tommy. Although I wonder why he never contacted me or never tried to visit me in hospital. I think of some of the girls I used to fancy like Daniella and Aoife; they all pale in comparison to Stephanie. I would do anything to be with her right now.

Henson nods. "I wish you all the best," he says, then we all leave.

Later, Dad visits. He sits comfortably on the sofa of the family room while I sit in an armchair.

He smiles. "I've good news. I've started going to Alcoholics Anonymous again and your Mum and I hope to do some marriage counselling in the future, once I get off the drink. So, things are getting better."

What do you think? Should I forgive and forget? It sounds good but we've been down this avenue before where he has tried to turn over a new leaf and it always ends up with him being worse than before.

There is an awkward silence that makes him smile then shake his head with a slight grin.

"Niall, how did we ever find ourselves here, in a mental hospital. I always had high hopes for you. If only you had been more like the people of antiquity or the saints of Christendom."

I sigh loudly. I've just simply had enough of listening to all this. "Dad, you're always looking back to the ancients of antiquity. You think that there was some kind of golden age where traditional values of honour were upheld and if we can only go back to those days, we will solve all our modern problems. Well, I've a newsflash for you, the ancients and saints were just as messed up as what we are."

His eyes widen with his mouth open.

"Oh, come on, the very origin story of Rome is based on the idea of revenge and murder. How is that meant to be moral, virtuous or conducive to my mental health. And didn't Saint Augustine describe the church of his day as a whore."

Dad sits back to regain his composure, his eyes now bulging. "Niall, I always gave you a strict upbringing because I knew you had potential to achieve great things."

"I don't want my life to be determined by dead Roman heroes, I want to be able to figure out things myself?"

"It's your cultural identity. You can't hide from who you are."

I shrug. "I decide who I am, not you or anybody from the past."

"But tradition ..."

"Screw tradition," I say, making Dad's face jar slightly. "Look, you never gave me the space to think for myself and come to my own conclusions about life."

Dad tuts. "Of course, I did."

"No, you only ever encouraged me to think the way you thought. I never was allowed to explore other viewpoints and other ways of life to see whether your truth was the real truth."

Dad nods with a bowed head but says nothing.

"Haven't you ever wondered whether your obsession with antiquity messed up our lives?"

He still says nothing.

"I mean, look how you treat Mum."

"Niall, you know it's the drink that does that."

I roll my eyes. "I know," I agree with a raised voice. "You hit the bottle when you lost your academic chair when you realised you were rubbish at everything else in life."

His eyes narrow and he points the finger at me. "I was a

MANIC

fantastic lecturer," he says, then recoils back slightly. "It was a shame the university took that away from me."

"And why did they take it away from you?"

He turns back to me, grimacing, tilting his head to one side and pursing his lips.

"Because ancient history doesn't have all the answers to life," I say.

He nods, dropping his shoulders and ducking his chin. "I only wanted to do what was best for you. To give you the cultured upbring I never had."

I grind my teeth. "The upbringing I never had? You beat us all to a pulp and you think it's compensated for by a cultured upbring."

"Niall, I'm sorry. I'm getting off the drink, I promise," he pleads with his hands held together.

He looks pathetic right now. "No. I've heard enough," I say, standing up with my hands up on my hips, frowning.

He stands up and stares at me for several moments then leaves. When the door closes, I sigh loudly, bow my head and close my eyes. When I open them, I see Dad's phone sticking out of the sofa cushions. I pick it up, wondering what to do with it. I decide to have a nosey at his recent messages.

The last person to message him on his WhatsApp is Jean Shepherd. Jean Shepherd? She's the farm vet. I press to see their conversation:

Jean: I had such a wonderful time with you last night. I hope to see you again soon.

Daniel: I enjoyed it too. Things have been hard with Siobhan and me. I'm glad to be able to talk to someone about it. You will always have a special place in my heart.

Jean: Don't mention it, you are always welcome in my home. Drop in whenever you need to. Xoxox.

What? Dad's having an affair?

I see him through the window of the corridor and chuck the phone back on the sofa before he opens the door.

"I think I must have left my phone," he says, searching around the room as he goes down on his knees. "Ah, there it is. Anyway," he says, turning to me, "get well soon. Deo volente."

Later, I have my lunch and go to the TV area. I sit, my legs

MARK BROWNLEE

shaking and then get up again to pace back and forth. "I'm going home," I shout in a loud voice. I'm awestruck when Stephanie comes into the canteen where she sits, glum-faced.

Stephanie? Here? like right now? I must be dreaming.

"Boy, I'm so glad you came to visit."

"I'm not here to visit you. I'm a patient," she yells.

I flinch yet strike up the courage to question her further. "What? What for? And what about you and Colin?" I ask.

"You'll be pleased to know Colin and I are through. But that's not why I took an overdose."

Okay, so yeah, I must admit I'm thrilled that Colin and her are through, but I'm horrified that she tried to OD.

"An overdose? Do you want to talk about it?"

"Why? Just so you can take advantage of me – the poor little Stephanie O'Reilly falls into the arms of Niall Alexander. You're just like all the other guys. I'd prefer it if you just leave me alone."

"Sorry, I only wanted to help you."

Honestly, I mean, I really care about her. I always have. Why can't she see that?

"I don't need your help. So, why don't you leave me alone by kindly buggering off."

I let out a sigh and go to my room. My shoulders fall and I scream as loud as my lungs allow before plunging onto my bed in an attempt to find some solace. Stephanie is not the one for me, even when she is free and single. I try to find a comfortable position but this ward isn't just like Purgatory – some waiting point for something better – but now it's a living Hell that is just getting worse. I long to be back home where I will be free to do my own thing. I suddenly leap up from my bed and run out of the room to the staff base where I bang on the door with my fist until one of the nurses responds.

"Where is Henson?" I shout.

"He's out."

"Tell him I want to go home now. I've had enough of this place."

The other nurse in the room is listening, as well as a consultant in a black pinstripe suit and pink tie who sits at a computer monitor. The figure is unknown to me – a man in his

MANIC

fifties, well-groomed and clean-shaven, having an uncanny resemblance to the President, James Edwards. I stare at him. He stares back at me.

"What are you doing here, you American scumbag? You've no interest in seeing me get any better. You just want to poke and prod me with a stick at your pleasure."

He doesn't respond, so I continue. "You abandoned me before I was put into the seclusion room. That's the last time I will turn to you for wisdom or advice."

He has a thin red book with the words WRAP programme at the top of it. He must be reading the book and my file. "Oh, so you think I need some programme to set me straight. Here is my programme." I stick up my middle finger at him and then turn and walk back to my room. Then a random thought festers in my head, and my heart races.

"Mum, why did you have to take all that abuse? It would have been better for all of us if you'd left him."

A nurse stands nearby, undaunted by my actions. I slowly regain my composure and glance up at Stephanie who is watching me, eyes narrow and mouth open. She says nothing.

I receive two blue-coloured tablets in a tiny container. After downing them with water from a plastic cup, I go back to my room and remain there, even during mealtime. I can't face Stephanie or anybody for that matter. I lie on my bed all evening, gazing aimlessly up at the ceiling. I don't go to the medicine room like the other patients but wait for a knock on the door. It's Christine who takes me to receive my medication. After I make my way back to my room, my stare locks onto Stephanie's, walking the other way. We both give each other looks of recognition without stopping, and continue on our paths.

26

REVELATIONS

Friday 3rd April

wake up after a bad night's sleep and reflect on my behaviour from the previous day. Has Stephanie now completely snubbed me? Has she given me the cold shoulder for good?

Although I want to, the reality is I can't hide in my room forever. I'll have to face her, so I pull back the covers and stand barefoot on the floor. I go to my wardrobe where, after several moments of hesitation, I decide what to wear, putting on a pair of burgundy chinos, red converse shoes and a white t-shirt. I enter the toilet to see how I look, and if I can make any improvements. I comb my long hair and brush my teeth. Then I shave, leaving a smooth finish to my face. If I'm about to be dissed by an absolute babe for being mad, at least I'll go down as a well-groomed madman.

MANIC

It's almost breakfast time, so I make my way to the canteen. The patients in line include Stephanie and Colin, although they keep their distance from each other. The shutter of the hatch soon rises then the cook starts pouring porridge into empty bowls and serves toast. Each patient gets their meal and takes their seat. Since I'm last in the queue, I have less choice about where to sit and I end up at a table on my own. I eat my porridge until I become bored so I get up from my table, go over to the trolley, neatly stack my bowl, and place the dirty cutlery in the container. Then I go over to Stephanie's table as a seat has become free.

"Hey. How have you been keeping?" I ask.

She immediately leaves the table. Then, before I can get up to go after her, Colin comes and sits with me. Colin? He's the last person I want to be with right now even though it feels like everybody is giving me the cold shoulder. Who else can I talk to?

"How are you, Niall?"

"Surviving," I reply, fist clenched and teeth gritted. It takes every ounce of my being not to punch him in the face. For some reason, I relax and ask him civilly, "Why are you being nice to me for a change?"

"I was wrong, Niall. Wrong about Stephanie and wrong to treat you the way I did."

"Ah, you sure you're alright?" I ask, glaring at him.

He laughs. "I could be better. Still, things could be worse. I was worried about you back in March when they transferred you and last night you appeared distressed. I hope you're okay now."

My jaw drops. Since when has Colin given a toss about my well-being? I continue our conversation, but I'm on my guard.

"I'm a lot better than what I was. Yourself?" I ask.

"Not too bad. I don't want to complain; it only makes the situation worse. I took an overdose of paracetamol when Stephanie dumped me and what do you know, I'm here now."

So that's why he's being nice to me. He wants to make sure I don't get her after she dumped him.

"That's why we are all here," I say.

"That's true. At least I'm better now."

MARK BROWNLEE

"What about Stephanie? She seems to have it all together," I ask, hoping Colin's emotions will get the better of him and he'll tell me something about why she's here.

"Oh yeah, she can give that impression," he says cynically. "She has that strong, confident demeanour. But I've witnessed her vulnerable moments," he says, probably delighting at her misfortune.

"What's her story?"

"Clinical depression with a bit of cutting on the side," he sneers.

Of course, she always wears long-sleeved tops to cover her arms.

"About a month ago, I found her hunkered down on her knees crying, 'I can't go on, Colin I can't go on,'" he says, mocking Stephanie. "That was the first time I'd seen her in that state. She would hide it from everybody. Thankfully, I found out soon enough. She's damaged goods. Take my advice and leave her alone."

Heat rushes through my body and I tense up. "I don't exactly have much choice since she's giving me the cold shoulder."

"Trust me, mate. Consider it a blessing. Oh, and by the way, they say your illness is the best one to have because at least you get the high. I'd sell my kidneys if I could have it instead of my condition."

"Maybe. But it's insufferable for everybody else who has to deal with all the erratic behaviour."

"I guess. There is no point wanting to walk in another person's shoes. You're better trying to accept your own."

Since when has Colin been a source of wisdom and insight?

"I have to say, Colin, you seem so able to be content with your condition."

"I've found it's the best way to be, whatever the situation."

"You're right, yet it's hard in every situation."

We finish talking. Jim exits the occupational therapy room and walks into the canteen and sees us.

"I was wondering if the two of you would like to do some

MANIC

cooking in the kitchen facilities, outside the ward?" he says, with his arms folded casually. "We're making fifteens. Fairly straightforward; very little can go wrong. So, are you two boys up for it?"

"Sure," we agree.

"Great! I'll round the troops up."

He turns around as Stephanie comes along the hallway. He asks if she's interested in cooking, and surprisingly, she nods. Soon other patients walk to the main entrance and we wait for Jim to lead the way. Once we're at the front of the hospital, memories of my escape from the ward floods back to me. I stride along the corridor at the same pace as everyone else yet slighter faster than the more medicated patients.

We draw near the exit of the hospital at the end of the corridor. If I want to, I could escape, but there's no gain in this. More than likely I'll be brought back in by members of staff, and my stay will probably be extended. I turn right, into another corridor and then into a small area where everyone stands before we go in.

Here, the walls and floor are grey. Large windows allow lots of natural light to shine in, a contrast to the murky orange light I experienced in the seclusion room, which was far more foreboding and disturbing. On our immediate right is a computer room which has a large bookshelf containing mostly works of bestselling fiction and sports biographies. Straight in front of us is the gym. It has weights and bikes as well as running and rowing machines. On our left is the kitchen. Jim stands outside peering through the window then he opens the door and invites us in.

We enter and assemble in the middle of the kitchen. Jim places bags of ingredients on the worksurfaces then he turns to us.

"Get into pairs."

Everyone pairs up. I look at Stephanie who frowns at me. Yet, somehow, I muster the courage to ask her to be my partner. Her face remains emotionless but she gently nods. Colin pairs up with Christopher who, yesterday, managed to become the first patient ever to beat Stephanie in a game of table tennis. Yet he never got a kiss.

MARK BROWNLEE

Once everyone is in a pair, Jim gives us instructions on how to make fifteens, then we start. Stephanie and I work in silence until after a while, I nudge her.

"Jim certainly knows his way around a kitchen."

My heart races when I see something I haven't seen in a while – her smile. Then, turning her head slightly, she points a wooden spoon at me.

"It's where the modern man belongs."

I tilt my head back and laugh. "I wasn't expecting to be caught up in a row on gender politics."

"What is your opinion on the role of women in the home, Niall?" she asks with her mouth open and eyes narrow.

I grin. "I guess in this day and age a man should have more of a role in the kitchen. But ..."

"But what?"

"I'm pretty hopeless at cooking and cleaning."

She huffs. "Typical guy! Claims he can't cook or clean so he can laze up on the couch and watch TV."

"Hey, let's not start stereotyping."

She nods with a smile. "True."

That smile of hers with her teeth showing is like the colour of vanilla ice cream. Aw, man. How I'd love to kiss her right now.

A quiet ensues between us as Stephanie continues to mix the ingredients in the bowl. Jim passes and says we have made the right consistency and the biscuit mix is ready to be rolled. We empty the bowl and sprinkle coconut flakes on the chopping board before rolling the mix over them. Once we've created a large roll, we put baking paper around it and then place it into the fridge to harden. While we wait, the patients use the gym and computer room in this section of the ward. Some remain in the kitchen and drink coffee together. The fire exit doors leading to the patio are opened to a cool but sunny day.

Stephanie and I stroll out onto the patio, each with a mug of coffee. The birch trees are gently blowing in the spring wind. There is a cool breeze that temporarily decreases the heat of the day before it's felt again. I turn to Stephanie. Her eyes are peering into space, her lips stiff and rigid.

MANIC

"Are you okay? It looks like something serious is on your mind."

"There is, but I don't think you would understand, Niall. I've been through a lot."

"So have I."

"I know. I ..."

"Stephanie, my dad's an alcoholic. He beats my mum and me to a pulp regularly, and despite my best efforts, I've never been able to stop him. It might surprise you how understanding I can be when it comes to tough times."

She gently pulls up the sleeves of her top, revealing many scars around her wrists. I place mine beside hers and for a moment we stare at each other. She turns away and sighs, cradling the mug of coffee in her lap. "To be honest, Niall, I don't even know where to begin."

"How did you first end up in a psych ward?"

She doesn't respond and takes another sip of her coffee.

I draw her out with another question. "Most people admitted to hospital go through a crisis moment. What was yours?"

"I took an overdose. It wasn't the first time."

"I'm sorry." I pause before speaking again. "Stephanie, you always seem to be one who has it all together."

"That's what everybody keeps saying but it couldn't be further from the truth. Something happened to me when I was sixteen."

"What? If you don't mind me asking."

"Over a year ago, I started a relationship with a male teacher in my school. At the time, I loved all the attention. Eventually, it progressed into a sexual relationship. Then, on one occasion, he forced himself upon me."

"He raped you?" I ask with a tightness in my chest, struggling to believe what I'm hearing.

"I'd prefer it if you didn't use that term."

"Sorry."

"Anyway, the whole incident came into the public domain, and the teacher lost his job. Everybody says it was his fault, he was in the wrong, but I blame myself for my part in the whole affair, and the incident still makes me feel ... violated

MARK BROWNLEE

and dirty. I felt so vulnerable, and no matter what people say, you blame yourself," she says, hiding the scars on her wrists.

"I don't know what to say. I've no idea what you must have been going through." Then again, a part of me thinks that I do. I often felt helpless and vulnerable when it came to my dad.

"I'm slowly coming to terms with it. Anyway, you haven't had it easy either. We were worried about you, Niall. I prayed for you," she says with reverence in her voice.

"Yeah, you're talking about the craziest person in this joint."

She laughs. "You're such a plank. But you're sweet at the same time." She opens her arms, embraces me. Then she gets up to leave.

"Where are you going?" I mutter.

She giggles. "To the loo. Can you handle that, Niall?"

I smile. "Of course."

As I wait, Ramona comes to sit down beside me. She grins and says she wants to tell me something.

"Sure," I say.

"Niall, ever since I laid eyes on you, I've wanted you."

I frown. "Ramona … I, ah …"

Before I can finish my sentence, she goes right into my personal space and kisses me on the lips. Initially, I struggle and try to pull her off but she's not a bad kisser.

She's my second, and compared to my first with Stephanie, she's not that bad. I place my hand on the back of her head until we separate. When I open my eyes, she leaves almost immediately. Then I turn to a red-faced Stephanie, hands on her hips.

27

THE PERFECT GUY AND GIRL

Friday 3ʳᵈ April

Stephanie's pretty blue eyes both enchant and disturb me. She recoils from me.

"I'm sorry. I …"

She sighs. "Niall, I'm sorry. I'm sorry how I treated you. I'm sorry how I chose Colin over you. I never really knew what sort of guy you were. I never knew how understanding you could be. But Ramona? I mean, seriously?"

"I know, but she kissed me first."

"You still seemed to enjoy it."

"I'm sorry."

She stares at me then walks off. Okay, where are we right now? I kissed Ramona when I was interested in Stephanie, but I wasn't going out with Stephanie or anything so why am I in

MARK BROWNLEE

trouble? I really hope I haven't messed this up. I walk along the corridor to her room and open the door where she's lying on her side on the bed, with her back turned to me.

I'm sweating all over. "Ah. I … I was wondering if you wanted to play a game of chess?" I stutter.

Stephanie laughs like I've never heard her laugh before. "Why? Does it turn you on?"

"Only if I'm playing you."

"To be honest, I'm more of a draughts player but I'll give it a go. I must warn you, I'm not very good."

I nod with a release of tension. We take a seat around a table in the canteen. Arranging the pieces on the board, I ask Stephanie what colour she wants to play as. She says black. I go first and move the pawn in front of my rook, nearest my queen, two spaces forward. Stephanie moves a knight out. I move the pawn in front of my bishop, (queen side) one space. She moves her other knight. I move the pawn in front of my bishop (queen side). Then she kills my pawn in front of my rook with her queen. Checkmated in three moves.

I feel my sore muscles and a pain in my jaw as I try to avoid eye contact with Stephanie. "Ah, I'm such a stupid git."

"Hey, I will not let somebody crucify themselves with shame. What's the matter? We all win and lose. We all make mistakes, Niall. Even me."

"I know … it's … I wanted to impress you."

She sniggers. "By beating me in a game of chess? You don't have a clue about girls."

I sigh. "The very first day I met you, I fancied you, yet I knew you were completely out of my league. I had to put on a mask that I was some grand Julius Caesar or Michael Collins."

Stephanie laughs. "Niall, both Collins and Caesar were assassinated for being great and grand. I prefer an ordinary guy who will always be there for me," she says, her voice rising at the end.

"You can still be great and not get assassinated. Don't forget the saviour of the Roman Republic, Publius Cornelius Scipio Africanus."

She sighs. "Niall, I've never heard of Pubby Corny Skippy Afrocactus. I'm sure he was a pretentious git."

MANIC

I frown. "How can you say he was a pretentious git if you've never heard of him?"

"Because he has four names. Any man who thinks he needs four names is overcompensating."

My head tilts to one side and I rub the back of my neck. "I want to be Superman."

Yeah, I know that sounds pathetic but at least I am being honest with her.

"Screw Superman. Niall, I like you for who you are, faults and all."

Like? What does she mean by like? Like, love like?

Stephanie continues. "Is that enough?"

I'm still processing whether she might love me. Is that like liking somebody like chocolate or is there something more to it than like friendship? Can I even entertain the idea that she means the romantic stuff? In regard to all that loving yourself stuff, I'm not sure.

"Well?" she adds, tilting her face slightly forward.

I shake my head slightly. "I don't know."

"Let's play a game of table tennis."

"I'm not really in the mood."

"That bad? What if I was to say my little kiss was still on offer if you win."

You'd think I would be up for it when she mentions the word 'kiss' in her sentence but I'm not.

"I'll probably lose like the last time and you'll probably get me to kiss another guy."

She folds her arms. "I won't."

"Christopher beat you. You never kissed him."

She rolls her eyes upwards and huffs. "That's because I never agreed to kiss him if he won as I did with you and Colin."

There is a tightness in my throat. "I'll still lose. You're too good."

"We all have good days and bad days," she says with a wink.

So, I agree.

We make our way into the foyer to the table. We both grab our bats. She swings her bat from side to side. Does she want to play me or does she want to kiss? Maybe both.

204

MARK BROWNLEE

"Okay," she says. "If you win, you get to kiss me. If I win, you'll have to kiss the lid of the bin."

"I thought you were trying to persuade me to play table tennis. Kissing the bin isn't a desirable prospect."

"Kissing me is. Besides, I'll go easy on you."

She's going easy on me. Maybe I stand a chance.

"Best out of three games up to twenty-one," she says.

"Sure."

We rally for a time. Jeez, but she's breathtaking, by which I mean she's literally taking the breath from me. Look at her. Her long flowery dress – enticing – . I can't help but check her out. Her denim jacket is ripped. It's like she's not even trying to be sexy with her wavy unstraightened hair and no makeup.

Somehow, must be by sheer fluke, I win the rally and serve first. I strike the ball; Stephanie hits it back and gets the first point. The ball goes over and back again. Over and over, point after point. This is a workout. She ends up slaughtering me.

"Fancy another?" she says and for a moment I think she's asking if I fancy someone else here. No! No, of course I don't Stephanie. You're the only one that makes me feel like this.

Maybe I can redeem myself with the second match. Is she not meant to be going easy on me? Or was she just spouting empty words earlier? She's looking at me now and there's a smile twitching at her lips. What's she thinking? Whatever it was behind that smile, the second match finishes and I scrape a win by a few points. Not bad, Niall. Not bad. Hey, you could probably go pro.

We start the final match, and although I'm not being a bad player, I'm no match for Stephanie when she's at her best. However, the tide turns in my favour and I'm sitting on twenty; Stephanie on eighteen. I need one more point to win this and kiss her. I can't. The nerves and pressure are starting to get to me. Stephanie seems to notice and smiles.

"Remember, this is me going easy on you."

I bounce the ball on her side of the table; it comes straight back at me like a bullet. Somehow, I hit it again. Stephanie responds and gets the point.

"Twenty, nineteen," I say, still shaking and sweating all

MANIC

over. Come on, Niall. Pull yourself together.

My service and I make a complete hash of it.

"Second serve." I hit it and the ball goes over the netting. It comes straight back before I can say 'deuce'.

I pick up the ball, and by nothing short of a miracle, I gain advantage in deuce. This is my last chance. I can't mess this up. I have to get this point. Standing in position, ready to hit the ball, I pause. My pulse is racing and the sound of my heartbeat is thrashing in my ears. Am I experiencing some form of shell shock from all her explosive aces? This doesn't go unnoticed by Stephanie.

"Come on, Niall. You can't bottle at this point."

I go to hit the ball but hesitate slightly so that it hits the central netting. "Second serve."

No, for real, this is my last chance. I can't mess this up. I've got to do this. Come on, you can do it.

I hit the ball. Thank goodness it goes over the central netting and bounces once on Stephanie's side of the table. I prepare for the inevitable strike of retaliation. It never comes. The ball bounces a second time and then third and then rolls off the table. I frown and stare at a smiling Stephanie.

"Looks like you'll be getting that kiss."

I freeze. What has happened? My heart rate suddenly picks up and there is an expanding feeling in my chest. She slowly walks over to me. The click of her footsteps on the floor and her pale cream face, her peachy lips, her lush ginger hair and those enchanting blue eyes that enthral me. She's getting closer. No, wait. Is she going to? No, she can't. Will she? She's even closer. Yep, she's now in my personal space, which means she's in kissing distance. No, she would never … She does. She grabs my collar and kisses me on the lips. I try to reciprocate with my kiss back but she recoils slightly, probably because I'm too eager.

"Stephanie?"

She smiles. "Yes."

"Before I came into the hospital, during my last day of school before the Christmas holidays, I was sitting in a history class when the teacher was out. All the girls started discussing with each other about what they would like to have in a guy.

206

They completely forgot I was there. The teacher was away for such a long time so they wrote down the attributes on the board. They drew a spider diagram with the words 'the perfect man' in the middle and all the characteristics around it.

It made me think of what characteristics would make the perfect girl. So, when I got home, I wrote about all the girls I'd fancied in my life, to form the perfect ideal. I ended up with a list poem I planned to send to Christa Edwards because I thought it best summed her up. The more I think about it, it sums up you. I learnt it off by heart."

"Okay, let's hear it. What's the title of your poem?"

"The perfect girl."

Stephanie laughs. "No surprises there."

"The Perfect Girl
Is there a girl out there for me?
one who has
the beauty of Christa
the fire of Daniella
the intellect of Maria
the warmth of Catherine
the helpfulness of Mary
the laughter of Brigid
the boldness of Kiera
the determination of Caitlin
the resourcefulness of Kathleen
the diligence of Aoife
the patience of Eimear
and the industry of Fiona.
I have not found her
at least not yet."

"Niall, I have a confession to make. I've also written a list poem similar to your own. I wrote it when I was like fifteen so it doesn't exactly ring true now. How did it go again? ... yeah:

Is there a guy out there for me?
someone who is
handsome, but never vain
athletic, but not Jocky
tall, but not ginormous
intelligent, but never nerdy

MANIC

well-read, but not bookish
sensitive, but never neurotic
strong, but not steroidal
leading, but never tyrannical
articulate, but never wordy
thoughtful, but never aloof
wise, but not a wise guy
supportive, but never clingy
empathetic, but not soft
romantic, but never effeminate
I've never found him
and I know I never will."

My jaw drops. "So, I'm not the perfect guy?"

"No. Nobody is."

"I thought you liked me."

"Niall, I do. The more I think about it, I might actually love you, for real."

I can't believe what I'm hearing. There is a tingling in my skin. Euphoria is flowing through my veins and there is a fluttery feeling in my belly. Yet there is still a question on my mind.

"Why? You know everything that's wrong with me."

I mean she knows I'm a messed up dirtbag. What does she see in me that I don't?

"That's the difference between love and infatuation. Infatuation is thinking somebody is perfect. Love knows somebody isn't but loves them anyway."

I stare at her.

"You're sweet," she says, holding a smile. "I want to give you something."

"Ah, that's very nice of you. What is it?"

"It's a surprise. I'm only going to give it to you in my room."

"Oh."

My thoughts freeze, then race, wondering what it could be. She gets up from her seat and soon after, so do I. We make our way back to the ward with Jim and the others. We are in the canteen area, Stephanie paces ever so slightly faster in front of me. She turns to me, flicking her long hair back as she pulls my hand. It becomes clear what the gift she is going to give to me is. I'm tingling all over and I'm breathless. I grasp her smooth and delicate hand. We walk, and she occasionally turns and smiles. My heartbeat speeds up. There's a rush of blood to my head and other areas of my body.

We enter her room and she turns and bends her right knee and rests her foot against the wall while also leaning her back on it. She smiles as her eyes run to mine. Our gazes are fixed on each other, and for a time there's nothing but silence. Can this be happening? I marvel at her beautiful face, like a work of art, her brow without a wrinkle. Her eyebrows form the great borders of her eyes, her long eyelashes and light blue eyes that are like two beacons of warm light at the top of the tower that's her nose. Then there are her lips which look so succulent in texture that I long to kiss them again.

It's her who takes the initial act of faith as her foot drops from the wall. Her eyes close as she projects her face upwards with lips clenched. I respond. With my neck tilted forward, eyes closed and mouth clenched, I place my right hand on her cheek. Our lips clasp to one another. We hold the same pose for what seems like hours yet it's only seconds. We keep kissing each other, our hands repositioning without our lips losing contact. Then, as we both stand, Stephanie pulls my chest into hers. Her hands rest at my sides as we continue to kiss.

Eventually, we do part, and we open our eyes. Our lips come together and there is an opening as Stephanie's tongue goes into my mouth where it's kindly greeted by my own. Each muscle caresses one another. My hands hold her tightly as my heart tingles, my head is full of ecstasy, and my loins are full of stiffness. Soon, the two of us are out of breath, and so our faces part once again. We continue to gaze at one another with broad smiles.

"I've found the perfect girl."

Stephanie smiles. "I can't say I've found the perfect guy. But that's okay."

28

LEAVING

Thursday 30th April

The day comes when I'm discharged from the hospital. That morning I have my breakfast with the other patients, but Stephanie isn't there.

"Hey, Jim. Do you know where Stephanie is?"

"Did you try her room?"

I feel a smile on my face as I go to her room and imagine making out with her again. There's a lightness in my chest. I'm floating as I walk with all the adrenaline rushing through me.

I knock on the door and open it slightly. "Stephanie?"

I opened the door further. The room's dark because the

curtains are pulled. I don't see anybody but I hear loud breathing. Then Stephanie sits up from the other side of her bed. I walk towards her. Her eyes are wide as she's hyperventilating.

"Stephanie?"

She doesn't reply.

I get closer and she's clenching and unclenching her fists. Her body is folded over, making her appear smaller. She moans and whimpers. Then she sits upright, shaking all over. I draw even closer. Her skin is sweaty and flushed, and she backs up against the corner of the room. She clutches her shoulders tight to try and stop the quaking. Soon, she controls her breathing and recovers. Her face is covered with her hand, unable to hold my stare.

She sighs loudly. "This is why I wanted somebody more stable than you. I thought you wouldn't be able to cope with my panic attacks. But actually, it was more than that. I thought you would never love me if you ever saw me this way."

I put my arms around her. "Stephanie, I'll always love you."

She nods with a slight smile.

"I was always conscious that you were infatuated with me. That you thought I was perfect, so, I tried my best to hide this from you. Do you think any less of me?"

What is she talking about? "Stephanie, I would never think any less of you."

There are circles under her eyes and her eyebrows draw together.

"Look, we've both got our problems and issues, but that's what makes our relationship so unique and special."

She bows her head and starts to cry. "I'm sorry, Niall, but I'm a total mess."

I embrace her for several moments then lift her head by her chin and stare into her eyes.

"I'm a total mess, too."

She says nothing. I squeeze her cheek and she laughs.

"Come on. I'm heading home today, and you're the only person I want to say goodbye to."

We leave her room holding hands. We reach the exit and I

MANIC

turn to her and, yes, you know exactly what I do. I have a proper good snog, French kissing, the whole works. Then I get a slap on my bicep. But it's not Stephanie. No, actually it's my mum.

"In public?" she says angrily.

I don't care.

There's a bittersweet taste to leaving. Of course, it's great to be leaving this place for good, yet it's sad to leave Stephanie behind.

"I promise to visit," I say, after a long embrace with her.

Mum and I arrive home and I look around the farm. I'm suddenly hit by a fresh smell of manure in my nostrils. The cows are lowing and the loose metal sheets of the sheds creak in the wind. I stretch out my arms and close my eyes.

"This will be mine and Stephanie's commune one day," I shout aloud.

"Well, at present, it's run by two greedy cutthroat capitalists."

I open my eyes – it's Conor – and I laugh.

We go into the house to the smell of potato and mince. The table is set and there are roses on it. Dad is wearing an apron, serving the meal. There's the hum of the extractor fan which sucks all the steam from the saucepans. This is strange for Dad and it makes everybody awkward. I mean, it's great he has stepped up to the occasion and done something for my discharge, yet I suspect a rat. Mum, Niamh, Conor and I sit down yet say nothing. When we're all served, Dad takes a seat.

"Now, I'll say grace."

Grace? We only say that on Sundays. Why are we doing it tonight?

"Our heavenly Father, we thank you for this meal we're about to eat. May you bless our fellowship and bring us closer together."

Okay, he never mentioned me in the prayer so it has nothing to do with my discharge. It must be something else. Why did he pray, "Bring us closer together"? Since when has he been a catalyst for that? No, really, what is going on right now?

Dad shovels food into his mouth with his fork like a

MARK BROWNLEE

starved rat. Everybody else is more reserved and eats more slowly. Then I know what all this is about. It's about his affair with Jean Shepherd. He regrets it and wants to tell Mum but needs to break it to her gently.

He smiles, taking another forkful and swallowing. "Mmmm, this is delicious."

Still, nobody else says anything. Man, this is like a paper cut to the eye.

We all finish and place our knives and forks in the middle of our plates. Is there any dessert? Dad is good tonight but he's probably not that good.

"Now that I have all of you around me, I would just like to say I have been making real progress in my AA group and ..."

"You're having an affair with Jean Shepherd," I butt in, wanting to get to the point. Now it's Dad's turn to be quiet. His mouth is wide open while everybody else gasps, particularly Mum.

"Is this true?" she asks.

"Well, I wanted it to come from my lips," he replies.

Mum places trembling fingers over her mouth. "I thought we were doing better."

"We are," Dad says, holding Mum's hand, "and that's why I wanted to tell all of you this all tonight. It was eating me up inside and I realised I wanted to come clean. No more secrets about the drink or Jean."

Mum recoils and her nostrils flare. "So, you think you can make a nice meal, tell me the news, say you're sorry, and everything will be okay?"

Wow, since when has Mum been this forward? No longer the doormat we always came to expect her to be.

"I ..." Dad mumbles. "I'm really sorry. It was a mistake and I want to make it up to you."

She slams her palm against the table and points the finger at Dad. "No. I've had to put up with your behaviour for too long."

"We're getting better," Dad protests weakly.

"I thought so too. I forgive you for the abuse because you were always under the influence but having an affair is completely different."

MANIC

Go Mum.

"Your children have always encouraged me to leave you for my own safety, but I always stayed because I thought I could save our marriage. But now you've thrown it back in my face."

"We still can. Please, Siobhan. I'm sorry. I need you," he pleads through sobs, tears in his eyes.

Mum tries to look away. This is hard for her. She needs to remain strong. Don't cave into his pleas.

Dad gets up and begs on his knees in front of her then grabs her wrists. Yet, she recoils in distress.

"Dad, leave her alone," I say, with a growing sense of alarm. "Dad, you're not drunk, so you've no excuse if you do something stupid."

Dad's face turns red and with a guttural roar he violently shakes Mum. She screams. Conor and I come to her aid and try to restrain Dad but it proves more difficult than expected, even with the two of us. He releases one of her wrists then slaps her in the face – it leaves a cut where his nail goes in. Conor and I try even harder to restrain him but he's consumed by hate. He lets go of her for a moment then squeezes her neck. If Conor and I don't do something fast, we'll be the witnesses of a murder scene.

I grab Dad's elbow with both my hands, and Conor does the same with Dad's other elbow. I squeeze but I can get him to let go of Mum. Suddenly, she's released and falls to the floor, holding her throat, gasping for air.

Dad stands at the other side of the room with Conor and me facing him, holding defensive stances.

He looks around the room, realises what he has done and he falls to his knees. "I'm sorry."

It seems like he is addressing all of us and not just Mum this time.

Once Mum has regained her composure, she steps in between Conor and me. "Daniel, this is the final straw. You're not even drunk and this is how you treat me. I say, good riddance. I really hope you find what you are looking for in Jean."

Dad says nothing. He's expressionless, yet from

everything that has happened tonight, he's really hurting. He's a broken man. He'd choose Mum over Jean in a heartbeat but things aren't going to end that way.

"I'm leaving you, Daniel. For good this time." She pauses, trying to judge how he feels from his expression. Dad is as a white as paper.

Mum clears her throat. "The children can decide who they want to live with, but at the end of the day, I have to look out for my own safety."

Mum leaves and is quickly joined by Niamh. Conor walks over and stands beside Dad. I should've guessed. Even though Conor doesn't think much of Dad, he's the golden child who's going to inherit the farm, and let's be honest, Dad couldn't run the place without him.

"Niall, you're going to have to choose," Conor says.

On paper, it seems like a straightforward decision. Choose between a loving mother or an abusive father. The countdown clock begins. Yet, at the end of the day, he's still my dad, my own flesh and blood. Despite everything I said before about being independent and determining my own future, there's no doubt I have been influenced by my dad's upbringing for better or worse. I'm about to make a decision that will change that forever.

"Sorry, Dad." Hang on, what am I sorry for after everything that has happened? I guess it just came out. "I want to live with Mum."

He says nothing.

"At least you've got Conor," I add before I turn and leave.

29

THE END OF THE BEGINNING

Friday 26th June

Niamh and I move out with Mum to a small three-bedroom house in Armagh. For Stephanie's eighteenth birthday, I book VIP tickets to a Spiffy Jenkins gig in the theatre. In the afternoon, Stephanie comes over to our house because I promise to give her a tour of the city, something I can tell I am going to enjoy more than her.

She sits in our rather plain and basic living room which we haven't put the Alexander signature mark on yet. Alexander? Will we be using that name for much longer? Mum's maiden name's Rafferty. We could revert to that.

Stephanie has her legs crossed, shifting slightly on the sofa. I bring in a bunch of orange roses similar to the ones I remember seeing in the palm house conservatory on Christmas

MARK BROWNLEE

Eve. I hope she'll like them. She takes them and immediately inhales their scent which brings a wide grin to her face. I stand, about to say something to her, but her gaze shifts as my mum enters the room.

"You must be Stephanie. I've heard so much about you. Would you like a drink? Tea? Coffee? Fizzy drink?"

"Tea, please."

Mum goes back into the kitchen and prepares our evening meal. She's probably the happiest I've seen her in a long time.

"Okay, a personal question, so take your time," I say.

"Oh, dear. I'm not looking forward to this," Stephanie says.

"Don't worry. You'll be fine. If you had to describe yourself as one animal, what would it be?"

I'm dying to know what she'll say because I have an animal in mind that will sum her up: a butterfly. Stephanie is pensive then turns to me.

"Okay, I've got one in mind."

"Good. Before you tell me, you've to think of the characteristics of that animal which best describe you."

"Okay."

"Let's hear it."

"A butterfly."

I can't believe it. "Really?"

"Yes."

"Why?"

"First, I gravitated more towards the idea of a fox. Yet the more I thought about it, the more I didn't want you to think of me that way. I wanted you to see me as what I am when I take my guard down, someone who's vulnerable and fragile, because I can be myself around you. What about you? What's your animal?"

"That's an interesting question. I can answer it with a little help from my friend, Teddy the turtle."

I pick up the turtle I won from the crane machine from behind the sofa and pretend it's whispering in my ear.

"What's that, Teddy? You say Niall thinks he's a turtle because he's introverted and likes his own space ... What's that? You say it's because of his difficult relationship with his

MANIC

dad."

Mum stops chopping carrots in the kitchen. Then a thought festers in my head that makes me cringe.

"What's wrong?" Stephanie asks.

"Oh, nothing," I lie, after wondering whether my relationship to Stephanie will end up as cold and abusive as my parents. Like father like son?

"Anyway," I say, "let's talk about something that will put a smile on our faces – the city of Armagh." Stephanie smiles as I throw the turtle back behind the sofa.

When we finish our tea, we head out and visit different parts of the city: the libraries, the planetarium, the museums and, of course, the cathedrals. I try my best to impress with my knowledge of the city. We go to the Catholic cathedral with its two spires which tower above everything else in the city. We enter and walk quietly around. She looks at the stations of the cross and the icons of saints. It's quiet. There are only about half a dozen people in total in the whole place. I sit in one of the pews; Stephanie follows hesitantly. I close my eyes and pray. Right now, I'm worrying if my relationship with Stephanie will last. I pray that God will make it last. I open my eyes. She's standing in the aisle, staring up at the nave. I attract her attention.

"Do you want to light a candle?"

She nods.

We walk to the back, and each of us lights a candle. We watch them flicker for a time before we leave. We pass the font on the way out and I turn to Stephanie.

"Hey, do you know how they make holy water?"

She shakes her head.

"They boil the Hell out of it."

She smiles but slaps me on the arm. As long as I can make her smile, this girl is a keeper.

"Standing here, looking at the other cathedral, always reminds me of how Rome was founded."

Stephanie rolls her eyes while I continue. "The story of Rome's founding comes when two brothers, Romulus and Remus, want to found the city on their own site or hill. Romulus kills Remus and then establishes his city. In Armagh,

MARK BROWNLEE

both Protestants and Catholics wanted to establish their church on different hills to make their claim over Saint Patrick, and the current demography is made up as a result. Also, the say Armagh is the city of seven hills, like Rome, although it doesn't actually have seven hills. Still we're currently in the most romantic city in the world."

"I'm sure Rome is more romantic. But in my humble opinion, I think Paris is the most romantic city in the world."

"It's more to do with who you are with than where you are."

She smiles and nods.

We have dinner together back at Mum's flat and then go to the Market Place Theatre where the gig is showing. We have front row seats, and the woman who is the supporting act isn't bad. She talked about how her husband said he was indecisive but wasn't sure, to which she replied, in all her years of marriage it's the only thing she can be sure of with him, that and his dirty laundry. A few of her jokes misfire, yet she gets a round of applause when she finishes. Then Spiffy runs on to a rapturous applause with his arms wide open. From the very beginning, he has everybody in stitches. My insides are sore.

"You know I'm a firm believer in marriage? After all, I've been married four times and the way I'm getting on, I'll soon make Henry VIII blush in his grave."

I laugh and then stop. What about Stephanie and me – will we last forever? Or will it end in heartache? I place my fingers through hers and she turns and smiles. Spiffy's main act finishes and he waves and leaves. Everybody keeps applauding until he comes out again for a final act. When he asks a volunteer from the audience, he gets them to read a comical dialogue. It's about how he unsuccessfully tried to ask a girl out over the phone when he was a teenager. It's hilarious. When everybody leaves, I turn to Stephanie.

"So, from what you've heard, who's better with the opposite sex? Spiffy or me?"

"You're bad but you're not as bad as Spiffy, although he's probably exaggerating for comic effect."

I scratch my skin and bite my lip before I ask her a question. "Stephanie, I was wondering how do you see us long

MANIC

term?" My muscles twitch waiting on her response.

"Niall, let's just take one day at a time," she says, then a smile glows on her face. "We're about to meet Spiffy Jenkins. Aren't you excited?" she asks, playfully punching me in the arm.

"I am."

We show our VIP tickets to a steward who leads us backstage to a small dressing room. We see Spiffy Jenkins sigh, his face in his hands. It seems out of character, yet he puts on a smile when he notices we're there.

"You must be the birthday girl, Stephanie. Or should I say, lady, now that you're eighteen?"

Stephanie giggles, flattered, while I smile awkwardly.

"So, is this your lucky man?"

"Yes, this is Niall. He's a big fan. When he was in the psych ward, he heard your voice in his head."

I forgot I'd told Stephanie that. Why did she have to say that? He'll probably think I'm proper mental now.

He smiles. "I have to listen to that voice inside my head twenty-four-seven, and I'm surprised I've never been chucked into a psych hospital. Nice to meet you, Niall."

I shake his hand.

"You've got a cross around your neck. Are you religious?"

I nod.

"Do you ever get voices from God?"

"Sometimes."

He smiles "Which was more prominent – mine or his?"

"Yours."

"Really? I'm kind of chuffed but also creeped out at the same time. So, you two are an item. Is this your first relationship?"

I nod as Stephanie shakes her head.

"Well, relationships are a bit like fat people, they rarely work out. I say that not to discourage you, but that you'll know the reality of what you're dealing with. They rarely work out because people don't realise the work that has to go in to make them work, yet when it does work, it's something beautiful. Ask my wife, she'll know, or maybe it's my lover. You're best asking both."

We chat with him for about fifteen minutes. We ask where he gets his ideas from and why he got into comedy. Then we walk home under the streetlights. I swing myself around lampposts which makes Stephanie laugh. My new favourite hobby is making her laugh. What if I'm not always able to do this? Despite all the things we have in common, sometimes it's like she's from Venus and I'm from Mars.

I go into the house with her and smile as I present her with a letter in the hallway.

"Open it," I say.

"You sure? It's addressed to you."

I nod.

She opens the letter and pulls out the piece of paper.

"Read it to me," I say.

"Dear Niall,

I greatly appreciate that you have taken the time to write to me and how you've kindly invited me to your home even if, by your own estimation, it's not overly grand or impressive.

I appreciate your information on Russia's military intentions. I will make my intelligence services aware of it.

In regard to Adam's ale, I have it in plenty of supply here. Concerning Adam's apple, every person on this earth has already tasted its bitterness.

Being an avid reader of Tolkien's works, I would jump at the chance of meeting someone who sees himself as Tom Bombadil, especially if he sees me as the great Théoden, king of Rohan. Unfortunately, I'm currently unavailable to visit you. Yet despite my high office, I am willing to serve you as much as I can by referring to what seems to be the main matter of why you are writing to me – a girl.

I must confess, I'm no guru on such matters. There are many pressing and demanding affairs of state I have to deal with on a daily basis yet the most perplexing moment of each day in the White House is when I get into bed at night with my wife.

I can read the minds of other heads of state pretty well and can predict their actions. I know the motivations of many of my political opponents and respond to them effectively. But despite thirty years of marriage, I still struggle to answer the

MANIC

question – what does my wife actually want?
Yours sincerely,
The President
of
The United States
of
America,
James Edwards."

She stares at the letter. "This is some kind of joke, right?"

I smile. "What makes you say that?"

"Well, the crayon drawing of the American eagle on the outside of the envelope raised my suspicions and the bizarre content in the letter."

I laugh hysterically.

"You're a great guy, Niall, but I don't think the President would ever have the time to write to you."

Stephanie looks at both sides of the envelope. I regain my composure and move closer to her.

"Well, Stephanie?"

"Well, what?"

"Can you solve mine and the President's conundrum: 'what do women actually want?' because it could make my life a whole lot easier."

She frowns. "How long have you got?"

I tilt my head closer to her and grin. "For you? A lifetime."

She turns to me and smiles. "Good, because that's what you'll need."

THE END

About the Author

Mark Brownlee is an Armagh-based writer and Mental Health support worker for the Southern Health and Social Care Trust. With lived experience from bipolar affective disorder, much of his writing touches on mental health. His poetry and flash fiction has been published in *The Bramley* and Poetry NI's *FourxFour*. *Manic* is his debut novel.

www.bluesmaniac.com

A c k n o w l e d g m e n t s

There are so many people I have to thank and acknowledge for helping me write, publish and get this work into the public domain. The first draft of this book was written in 2017 and was inspired by a six-month period I spent in Bluestone psychiatric hospital, Craigavon, from December 2014 to May 2015.

Thank you to everybody who supported me in whatever small way to get this novel to the final publication stage. It has taken me six years to get here. A large part of that time was me finding the confidence to put it out there.

To my editors, Nathan Elout-Armstrong and all of the people from Jericho Writers who played a role in improving the manuscript. To Harry Bingham and his very helpful self-publication course. To Debi Alper and the self-edit course, and my professional editors: Becky Hunter, Julie Hoyle and Louise Walters.

A special mention goes to Paul Maddern and the River Mill Writers Retreat. His support during the editing phase was critical to the final shape of the book. Oh yeah, and because his cooking skills and hospitality are fantastic.

Thank you to my friends and beta readers Darrell Stanley, Celine Holmes, Lorna Flanagan. And to Byddi Lee and Malachi Kelly for giving me the platforms of Flash Fiction Armagh and Abbey Lane Open Mics to give me the confidence to get my work into the public domain.

Thanks to all those individuals of support I have received from countless people along the way who I don't have the time to thank.

Since a large part of my writing and editing process took place in local cafes. I'd like to make honourable mentions to those I was in the most, the Craic'd Pot, Armagh, Cafe Nero, Armagh, Costa, Armagh and Dungannon.

Finally, to my family: Mum, Dad, Andrew, Rachel, Sarah, Esther and Lynn and their other halves. Most were present at that infamous Christmas of 2014, so they all have a fair idea of what this book is about without even reading it.

Printed by Amazon Italia Logistica S.r.l.
Torrazza Piemonte (TO), Italy